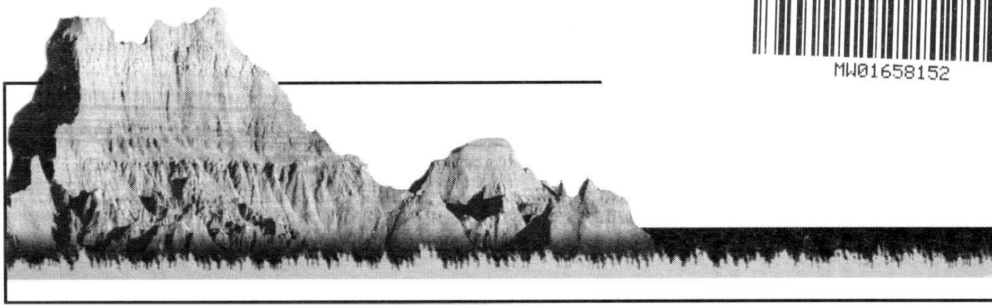

North Dakota

1960 to the Millennium

Kimberly K. Porter
University of North Dakota

KENDALL/HUNT PUBLISHING COMPANY
4050 Westmark Drive Dubuque, Iowa 52002

ISBN 978-0-7575-5641-8

Printed in the United States of America
10 9 8 7 6 5 4 3 2 1

Acknowledgments

The opportunity to acknowledge in print those who have helped to make your road just a bit smoother comes far too rarely in the academic world. How many books can a historian churn forth in a career? And how many of the innumerable contributors, both in large and small terms, can actually be mentioned without the gracious commentary appearing like a phone book? A noble attempt at recognizing those who have made this book possible follows.

My gratitude goes to many, including my research assistants Elisabeth Saunders and David Thompson who dug through newspapers, archives, and dusty collections of books, with nary a public complaint, and who searched the Web for arcane facts, figures, and photographs. They provided an enthusiasm that helped to keep this project alive at a couple of very exhausted moments.

My gratitude goes also to the students of History 220: History of North Dakota. Each semester they pose the questions, challenge the assertions, and offer new insights to the class, always wondering why we never get to the present day. Now, I promise that we will, or at least reasonably come close to it. If all else fails, you will at least have a text to provide the context for your lives in North Dakota.

My gratitude also goes to my colleagues at the University of North Dakota who suffered my perpetual running commentary on this volume, rarely hid from me, and generally offered thoughtful criticism. Of particular assistance was Dr. Gordon L. Iseminger, a scholar of Great Britain who has become a man of the plains.

On a personal level, I offer my gratitude to Linda M. Baeza, Stephanie Clark, Warren Porter, JoAnn Olson, and Kimberly Gregg. They know what they have contributed, and that is enough said. To quote someone who rarely comes to mind in discussions of North Dakota—Gertrude Stein—"if not, not."

As always, the errors are mine.

Kimberly K. Porter
Emerado, ND

Introduction

On November 6, 1958, Elwyn B. Robinson, Professor of History at the University of North Dakota, stood before his colleagues on the occasion of the seventy-fifth anniversary of the institution. Regarding his audience of "thoughtful people," he challenged them to consider: "What are the great themes of North Dakota history? How are they related to each other? How are they tied to the fundamental facts about the state?" Undoubtedly hearing no response to the rhetorical questions, he provided a carefully crafted argument. It focused upon six themes he believed to be essential to understanding the past, as well as the future of the state: remoteness, economic dependence, radicalism, dependence, adjustment, and the "Too-Much Mistake."[1]

Elwyn B. Robinson

Courtesy of the Elwyn B. Robinson Department of Special Collections, Chester Fritz Library, University of North Dakota.

A year had not passed when Robinson refined his thematic conceptualization of North Dakota history with an essay simply titled: "Six Themes of North Dakota History." Little had changed since his presentation, except his assuredness in his thematic guideposts to the history of his adopted state.[2] All was in prelude to the book he had spent the majority of his career contemplating, researching, and writing.

At its appearance in 1966, *History of North Dakota* met with rave reviews. Assorted book reviewers described the volume as "absorbing," "fascinating," "astonishingly comprehensive," and "balanced." However, the more adept reviewers noted one additional factor: Robinson's work moved the concept of state history to new heights. Previously, state history had ofttimes met with derision in academic circles. However, upon a close reading of the text, reviewers observed that Robinson's work could be considered little less than a breakthrough in the genre.[3]

Reviewers from such diverse publications as *Arizona and the West*, the *Journal of American History*, the *American Historical Review*, and the *Journal of Economic History* noted that Robinson had broken the boundaries of traditional state history, not only by expanding his lens to the region, as well as to the nation, but also by including material more traditionally considered as anthropology, geography, economics, political science, and sociology. Rather than simply a narrative of events and individuals, Robinson worked from his interpretive framework of the six themes, grounded in the geographical realities of the state.[4]

Perhaps John Schlebecker most clearly articulated the true significance of Robinson's achievement. Writing for the *Journal of Economic History*, he observed: "This history could well be used as a model for other state histories. Practitioners of this art have produced some excellent work of late, but this is it, I think, the best so far." Declaring the *History of North Dakota* to be pathbreaking in the 1960s is one thing, to have it remain so in the first decade of the new millennium is quite another. Clearly Robinson has served the test of time.[5] Not so with the handful of other scholars who have attempted a comprehensive view of North Dakota.

Indeed, scarcely had North Dakota become a state when historians began their analysis of the region. In reality, Frank Hagerty commenced his inquiries in 1889, the very year of statehood. His *The Territory of Dakota, the State of North Dakota, the State of South Dakota: An Official Statistical, Historical and Political Abstract*, purported to be the first detailed examination of the lands that became North and South Dakota, as well as the northern state during its first months of existence. Chock-full of statistics regarding population, religion, school buildings, manufacturing, and the like, as well as the names of governmental officials, past and present, the text served the new state well as a reference tool, but offered no sense of interpretation.[6]

Barely had a decade of statehood passed when the anonymously authored *Compendium of History and Biography of North Dakota* appeared. In subscription volume of 1,410 pages, a mere 156 were devoted to the heritage of the state, the remainder being brief biographical sketches of the state's early success stories in the realms of politics, religion, agriculture, business, and so on. Within the context of the "history" portion of the compendium, covered topics included issues of economics, politics, the railroads, agriculture, and education. No social or cultural material filled the pages of the volume. No effort at interpretation could worry the inquiring reader.[7]

As the state developed, it indeed had a European American *history* that could be told. The first to attempt a comprehensive treatment of North Dakota's heritage was Colonel Clement A. Lounsberry, founder of the *Bismarck Tribune*. His three-volume series—*North Dakota: History and People, Outlines of American History*—covered the state's European American past from 1675 through 1916, clearly focusing upon the latter years of this span. Lounsberry's primary interests lay not in what would today be considered social or cultural history, but rather in the realm of the politics of the state, as well as its military affairs. A subscription series, the last two volumes served to provide detailed sketches of the state's political, agricultural, business, and clerical leaders.[8]

Clement Lounsberry

Courtesy Archives of Michigan.

In so much as Lounsberry attempted an interpretive framework, it could be declared from his Introduction: "More intensely interesting than a fairy tale is the story of the development of the great Northwest." History is henceforth a study in progress, predominantly focused upon the Europeans and European Americans who advanced their civilization upon the wild and barren grounds of North Dakota.[9]

Lewis Crawford's 1931 *History of North Dakota* clearly followed in the pathway broken by Lounsberry, as did the 1938 *North Dakota: A Guide to the Northern Prairie State* as prepared by workers for the Federal Writers Project of the Works Progress Administration. Both texts clung to the image of the sturdy pioneer and his placid wife forever peering west, carrying the accoutrements of Christian civilization, democratic government, and the steel plow to supplant the Native American farmer with her bison-blade hoe.[10]

Scholars of the mid-twentieth century turned their attention from the march of civilization's progress—and the great white men responsible for it—towards a more finely honed interpretive framework. Working in the 1940s, two histories of North Dakota materialized: Conrad W. Leifur's *Our State North Dakota* made its appearance in 1942, and quickly became the standard text for secondary schools in the Flickertail State. Also appearing in the 1940s, *Land of the Dacotahs* by Bruce Nelson offered an interpretation similar to that of Leifur. In both instances, the great man has slipped to the side, no longer marching forward under the simple guise of progress. He has been replaced in Leifur and Nelson's labors by the concept of economic betterment. Hence, although progress as progress lurks in the background, the state's history can best be told as individuals' efforts at self-improvement of the financial sort. Although produced somewhat later—1963—Erling Nicholai Rolfsrud's *The Story of North Dakota* adopted the same general interpretive framework.[11]

Then came Robinson, who turned the study of North Dakota history on its head. Indeed, following Robinson's new interpretive framework, no historian of the North Dakota experience—at least in its entirety—could afford to ignore the by-now infamous "six themes." And, to date, none has.

Writing in 1976, D. Jerome Tweton and Theodore B. Jelliff's North Dakota: *The Heritage of a People* remained true to the formula. In this volume aimed primarily at secondary school students, Robinson's themes were utilized "to explain the state's human history and to combine human aspirations with the requirements exacted by the plains environment."[12]

Contemporaneous with Tweton and Jelliff came *North Dakota: A History* by Robert P. Wilkins and Wynona Hutchette Wilkins. Written for an adult audience, and published as a part of the States and the Nation Series by the American Association for State and Local History for the nation's bicentennial, their work relied significantly upon the themes laid forth by Robinson, particularly with regard to the power of the natural environment and the impact of remoteness upon the citizenry of the state. They noted, as well, in their introduction that their labors were in no way meant to be heroic in scope, but rather "working within the limits of the editors," they had been forced to more tightly focus upon "the people who have devoted a century to it and to interpret the unique political experiments undertaken here." Thus, *North Dakota: A History* could be counted as one step away from Robinson as not relying exclusively upon his themes to tell the state's history, but also a step backward to reliance upon political narrative.[13]

Also a product of the 1970s was Jelliff's solo effort: *North Dakota: A Living Legacy.* Aimed towards the secondary school reader, the text broke no new ground, relying upon Robinson to build the image of a "unique North Dakota character," one typified by independence tempered by interdependence, shy pride, friendly openness, and a personal calmness that belies a spirit of courage and faith in the future of North Dakota.[14]

The foregoing focus upon volumes that attempt to provide comprehensive coverage of North Dakota's history is not to suggest that volumes related to a specific corner of its heritage have not been produced. A bibliography of such works would include explorations of African Americans in North Dakota, a study of the Gordon Kahl murders, an examination of the Farmers Union, as well as detailed discussions of mining. Moreover, the significant figures of North Dakota's heritage have not been ignored. Biographies, both in book and article form, exist for many governors, as well as legislators, businessmen, sports figures, and educators. North Dakota's tribal populations have been studied in depth, as have its natural environment, its political institutions, its key cities, and so much more.[15]

The looming question must then be asked: "What does *North Dakota: 1960 to the Millennium* offer that has not already been provided by previous scholars?" or "Why do we need another study of a low population state in the infamous 'flyover country'?"

The answer is relatively brief. In this volume, I do not attempt to be comprehensive. The material "facts" of North Dakota from its pre-territorial days to the 1950s have been covered and covered with great depth and from a variety of perspectives with a variety of audiences in mind. *North Dakota: 1960 to the Millennium* provides a detailed exploration of the years following Elwyn Robinson's classic history of the state, which drew to its conclusions in the early 1960s. *North Dakota: 1960 to the Millennium* will not therefore concern itself in the years before 1960, excepting as prelude.

More importantly, this text offers a new framework by which to examine North Dakota over the last 50 years. That framework, which relies to an extent upon the work of Robinson, is grounded in an exploration of the rising role of the federal government in state affairs, recognition of the power of the natural environment, and an understanding of the demographics and economics that drive the whole.

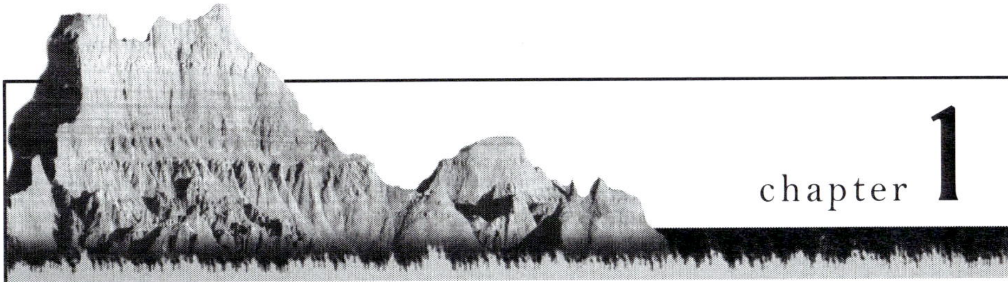

chapter 1

PRELUDE
The 1950s

Throughout much of their history, North Dakotans have clung to an image of themselves as an independent lot. In his masterful *History of North Dakota*, Elwyn Robinson noted that this is somewhat less the case than more. In the scenarios that Robinson uses to uphold his thematic view of North Dakota's dependence, those who would seek to rob the state of its independence are influences from the outside: banks, railroads, insurance companies, lumber firms, and industrial concerns.[16]

In his introduction to the second edition of *History of North Dakota*, D. Jerome Tweton, himself a longtime scholar of the North Dakota scene,[17] expands upon the theme of dependence as developed by Robinson. Due to the remoteness, geographic as well as ideological, of the state from the sources of financial, political, cultural, and industrial power, its residents had grown to have not only a dependent mindset, but as well, a dependent reality.

In his summary of Robinson's work, Tweton observed that three forms of dependence could be readily identified in *History of North Dakota.* Initially, Native Americans became dependent upon European and European American fur traders for goods they could not produce, on goods they had become reliant: guns, ammunition, metal traps, pots, vermillion dye, and other such manufactured products. Access to the markets that could readily supply these goods came under the control of the white traders.[18]

Soon, however, the white trader fell way to the white settler, intent upon carving a farm and a future from the lands that were to become the thirty-ninth state. Their dependence upon the firms and factories of the East came near to being complete. Beyond the purchase of necessary goods in the form of plows, windmills, sawn lumber, and barbed wire, among other manufactured goods, came the brutal fact that the East also held the financial keys to the plainsman's success.

Not only was the North Dakota farmer dependent upon the industrial powers of the East, he was also dependent upon the markets of the massive cities for the purchase of his wheat and his beef. Before his grain, in particular, could find a marketplace, however, came the most potent factor of all: the railroads. The Northern Pacific, which crossed the territory for a full decade before statehood, set much of the tone, demanding a subservience that galled quite painfully. The railroads, including as well the Great Northern, set the rates for hauling grain, discriminating at will among shippers, often smiling most endearingly upon their own line elevators to the detriment of privately held endeavors.

Moreover, the Minneapolis flour mills to which the railroads delivered the region's wheat also took their toll upon the farmers of northern Dakota Territory. Sales of wheat rose rapidly as the new spring wheat country came into production over the course of the 1870s and 1880s. In 1874, for example, the Northern Pacific carried 144,000 bushels of wheat to the Twin Cities millers. A decade later, the railway carried 5,700,000 bushels of wheat to the millers at the Falls of St. Anthony. The line that would later become the Great Northern, the St. Paul, Minneapolis, and Manitoba, carried 2,300,000 bushels of wheat in 1874 and in 1884, the same line carried 20,700,000 bushels.[19]

With little competition for rail service and little as well for the flour millers, Dakota farmers clearly felt dependent upon Eastern interests. They were further put upon by a grain grading system that favored the distant terminal markets that determined the quality of the grain delivered without the input of those who had grown it. Almost miraculously, grain that was first judged to be of lower standards could be pooled with small quantities of grain judged to be of higher quality, elevating the entire pool to a superior grade, ultimately benefiting the grain dealers, but not the farmers. Short measures on grains also found farmers fuming. In one year, Duluth's dealers sold more than two and a half million bushels of wheat more than they had collectively purchased.[20]

Of lesser concern, but not without its detractors was the power of the Eastern-based federal government. Responsible for such measures as the Homestead Act (1862), the Morrill Land Grant College Act (1862), the Pacific Railway Act (1862), and the Northern Pacific Railway Act (1864), government for most had a benign, if not positive, impact on their lives. Slowly though, power of the government grew: Conscripted soldiers found themselves in the trenches of European battlefields, Federal Reserve Banks arranged for low-interest loans on agricultural expenses, Prohibition became the law of the land, and interstate cooperative endeavors became legal under the terms of the Capper-Volstead Act.

The 1930s witnessed the largest-to-date expansion of the federal government with a flood of relief measures collectively known as the New Deal and targeted towards ending the Great Depression. Over the course of the 1930s, alphabet agencies provided relief to the state's nearly 700,000 residents when the coffers of state, county, city, and charitable agencies had run dry. Civilian Conservation Corps boys—some 12,000 strong—built parks and picnic shelters, planted trees, and constructed dams.[21]

The Federal Emergency Relief Administration, active from 1933 through 1935, "built 114 dams, 34 wells, 60 bridges, 2,300 miles of streets and highways, 986 sanitary privies, 70 public buildings, 14 swimming pools, 11 playgrounds, 88 tennis courts, 32 golf courses, 108 skating rinks, 40 baseball diamonds, 36 airports, and 23 parks."[22]

Taking into consideration relief programs and payments made to farmers under the assorted farm programs of the 1930s, the federal government spent about $266,000,000 in North Dakota alone during the Great Depression. Still, as Robinson noted, the great charity of the nation did not make the residents of North Dakota grateful to the Democratic Party and its standard bearer Franklin Delano Roosevelt. Rather, during the depths of the Depression, citizens twice voted to support FDR (1932 and 1936)[23] and then returned to the Republican column in 1940, voting for Wendell Willkie, 155,000 to

124,000. In 1944, despite the ongoing war, North Dakota's citizens again cast their ballots for the Republican candidate Thomas E. Dewey, 118,535 to Roosevelt's 100,144.[24]

The coming of the Second World War brought further federal involvement in the lives of North Dakota's citizenry. In October 1940, more than a year before the bombing of Pearl Harbor, North Dakota's 55 draft boards met to commence the registration of men under the Selective Service Act. Before the war's end, 145,000 men from 18 through 44, the age group susceptible to military conscription, had been registered. Of these men, 37,913 were drafted for service in one of the nation's military branches. Another 20,596 men volunteered for service. In addition, some 1,570 women volunteered for wartime service in the WAVES, WACS, and other temporary duty divisions of the military.[25] Of these men, 1,939 died, predominantly as members of the United States Army. With a death rate of 4.14 percent, compared to a death rate of 2.98 percent for the remainder of the United States, North Dakota offered up more than its share of human sacrifice. Undoubtedly the toll would have been significantly higher had not some 50,000 men received deferments in order to produce food for the war effort.[26]

Those men receiving deferments to remain on the farm or the ranch gave of themselves without stint to the war effort, urged on by the federal government at every turn. The return of rainfall to the plains and prairies of North Dakota allowed for the most significant crops to be raised since the end of the 1920s. For example, the 1941 crop produced 140,000,000 bushels of wheat with a resulting farm income of $233,000,000. Considering that from 1933 through 1940, North Dakota had not produced a wheat crop in excess of 100,000,000 bushels with the total wheat income often lagging below $2,300,000 per year, it seemed as if profit had finally returned to the agricultural sector.[27] The crops found a ready market, something farmers had not seen since the late 1920s. Indeed, rationing, not only of foodstuffs, but also of gasoline and tires, became the order of the day for North Dakotans, as well as all Americans.

The power of the federal government was felt not only in the effort to produce more food and to ration that which had been produced, but also in the need for additional laborers in the nation's defense plants. An estimated 50,000 men and women left the state's farms during the war to take up positions making airplanes, ships, parachutes, ammunition, and multitudes of additional war-related necessities. In response, farmers worked longer hours, utilized the latest available technology, and employed schoolchildren, townspeople, and college students in their fields and feedlots.[28] Farms also became larger during the war years, and lessened slightly in numbers, from 74,000 farms in 1940 to about 69,500 in 1945, growing from 513 acres to nearly 600 acres per operation. More and more farms and ranches crossed the bar to become operations of over one thousand acres.[29]

Not only did North Dakotans feel the power of the federal government on the farm front. A limited number of war contracts were let to North Dakotans in pursuit of the Allied victory. Despite the diligent labors of Governor John Moses, and his War Resources Committee, the state could only garner $9,600,000 of the $225,000,000,000 awarded, possibly the least of any state in the union. Those contracts granted generally focused on agricultural elements such as the processing plants built to dehydrate potatoes, eggs, meat, and milk.[30]

Not all federal activities in the state focused upon food production and preservation. North Dakotans also saw its government in action in the establishment of training facilities essential to an Allied victory. Men studied at the University of North Dakota in intensive engineering programs, while nearly 1,000 compatriots at the same institution gained instruction as Army Air Corps glider pilots throughout the war. Additionally, civilians learned aeronautics under the guidance of the United States Army Air Corps, while others gained valuable skills for their role in the Signal Corps, and still others learned basic medical training at the University of North Dakota, including a contingent of nurses.[31]

All North Dakotans rallied to the cause in some fashion or another. Literally tons of scrap metal moved from the junk heap to the nation's smelters, while housewives saved fat and children conducted paper drives. Given that the state was just emerging from the depths of the Great Depression and the agricultural depression that preceded it, North Dakotans purchased an astonishing $397,000,000 worth of war bonds. In one of the drives, North Dakota led the nation in per capita bond buying.[32]

More than any event preceding it, World War II made North Dakotans aware of their place within the federal structure, as well as the federal government's place within their individual lives. The role of the federal government would not decline over the remaining years of the century, but rather would only continue to grow. Also growing was the loss of youth to opportunities and needs lying outside the boundaries of the state.

Even before General Yoshijiro Umezu and Fleet Admiral Chester Nimitz, under the watchful eyes of General Douglas MacArthur, affixed their signatures to the instrument of surrender ending World War II in the Pacific Theater, it was clear that true peace would not prevail. Despite MacArthur's radio address from the deck of the *U.S.S. Missouri* calling for a permanent end to war, the relationship between the United States and the Union of Soviet Socialist Republics—the Russians—had deteriorated into what has become known as the Cold War. With each side entrenching itself and its allies in the global effort to contain or expand the influence of communism, a battle of wills backed up by weapons of mass destruction began, leaving an indelible mark not only upon the nations, but also upon their component states. North Dakota in particular would feel the impact of potential nuclear annihilation, perhaps more than any other state.

In the immediate aftermath of the war, the United States held a technological advantage over the Soviets with regard to nuclear technology, and assumed it would do so for many years. Hence, from 1945 through the autumn of 1949, strengthening the United States Air Force, or other branches of the military, did not seem an issue of the highest order. However, on September 23, 1949, Soviet Premier Vyachesov M. Molotov announced that the Russians had discovered the secret to the atomic bomb, quite literally decades before the American military-industrial complex considered this to be a possibility.[33] Overnight, the United States found itself having to prepare for the possibility of a Soviet airborne atomic attack.

By 1951, General Hoyt S. Vandenberg, Air Force Chief of Staff, revealed that an astounding 70 percent of Soviet bombers could achieve U.S.-based targets. And with the Soviets' ever-increasing attention to technological issues, that number could only be expected to grow in the coming years. Vandenberg, accordingly, with other members of the Joint Chiefs of Staff, proposed that the United States devote more attention and money to air defense technology and bases. It was recommended that the 42 air bases in the continental United States be expanded to at least 143 air bases, and in relatively short order. In 1953, President Harry Truman authorized a substantial increase to the Air Force, Army, and Navy's budgets. The Air Force had nearly $21 billion at its disposal.[34]

Quickly realizing that the shortest distance between two points is a straight line, North Dakotans soon rallied to the idea of defensive air bases. Clearly if the Russians chose the shortest route to the heartland of the United States, it would be via the North Pole. Senator Milton R. Young (R-ND) always eager to secure reelection turned his plentiful talents on the wooing of the United States Air Force to his home state. His courtship did not have to be all that arduous as others had quickly surmised as well that North Dakota presented one of the best options for scrambling the airplanes that would defend the nation.[35] A number of North Dakota communities made it clear that they would appreciate the opportunity to host an air force base, including Fargo, Bismarck, Grand Forks, Williston, Jamestown, Enderlin, Valley City, Underwood, and Minot, among others.[36]

Senator Milton R. Young

Institute for Regional Studies, NDSU, Fargo, ND. Used with permission.

Preliminary surveys undertaken in 1954 by the United States Air Force suggested that the Fargo and Bismarck areas would make satisfactory choices for new air bases. Indeed, the residents of the areas seemingly selected to host the bases began their celebrations early, contemplating the money that would pour into their towns with the construction of bases, as well as with the men and women who would come to serve these bases. Fargoans had been told by Lieutenant Colonel E. A. Munns, representing the director of installations for the Air Force, that a base in the community would mean "25 all-weather jet interceptors, 786 officers and men, hir[ing] 81 civilians, and hav[ing] a monthly payroll of approximately $225,000."[37] Unfortunately for Fargo and Bismarck, the celebrations began a bit too early; the deals were not sealed, and the Air Force continued to look for the best locations possible.

Over the space of a mere few weeks, both Fargo and Bismarck fell from the running. Fargoans could not see their way clear to spend thousands of dollars to expand the local airport—Hector Field—to the standards required by the Air Force, even if that land would secure the construction of a $7,055,000 base, and its continuing economic value to the community. Individuals at Bismarck were also hesitant to put forward thousands of dollars to secure an air base when, as with Fargo, the Air Force demanded an expansion of the local airport, or a donation of land suitable for the construction of a new combined airport/air base. In what appears to be a somewhat short-sighted venture, Bismarck fell from the list of contenders for a $7,558,000 base construction budget and ongoing economic growth for want of a few thousand dollars.[38]

The Air Force delegation continued its exploration of possible sites within the Flickertail State, finally settling upon the communities of Minot and Grand Forks, which were announced as the homes of the new bases on June 17, 1954. By no coincidence, that was the exact day the Senate passed the defense appropriations bill totaling $28,217,106,486. The site for the Minot base would be approximately 10 to 15 miles northwest of the Magic City, and the Grand Forks base would be located approximately 10 to 15 miles northwest of the community.[39]

Groundbreaking at Minot took place on July 12, 1955, shortly after local businessmen purchased the site of the future base for $50,000. Work quickly commenced and the United States Air Force activated the Air Defense Command 32nd Fighter Group on February 8, 1957. The 4136th Strategic Wing of the Strategic Air command arrived in September 1958, with the 906th Air Refueling Squadron assigned to Minot Air Force Base in the early spring of 1959.[40]

Siting the Grand Forks Air Force Base did not come quite so easily. Initially plans called for the base to be located north and west of the city near present-day Manvel. However, engineers quickly discovered that the soil would not support the planned construction. Accordingly a new location would need to be discerned. After a bit of haggling with local landowners, the Grand Forks Air Force Base came to be situated approximately 15 miles west of the city. The citizens of Grand Forks, eager to have an economic windfall in their own backyard, donated money towards the purchase of the 5,400-acre parcel. Construction began on the site on February 5, 1956, with the arrival of the first military personnel in January 1957, and the activation of the 478th Fighter Group.[41]

Shortly thereafter, the federal government activated the 4133rd Strategic Wing (Provisional) as a tenant of the Grand Forks Air Force base, meaning that the unit would serve as host for a fighter-interceptor squadron, an air defense sector operation, and a Strategic Air Command center. On December 15, 1959, the Grand Forks Air Defense Sector of the North American Air Defense Command (NORAD) became operational.[42] As never before, residents of North Dakota realized the power and the presence of the federal government in their lives.

Garrison Dam, in west-central North Dakota, also served as a bold reminder of the power of the federal government. The dam was born of conflicting plans. In 1942 W. G. Sloan of the Bureau of Reclamation argued that diverting water from below the Fort Peck Dam in Montana would allow for the irrigation of approximately one million acres of northwestern North Dakota. His plan also called for hydroelectric power to be generated from the dam's turbines. Shortly thereafter, Colonel Lewis A. Pick of the Army Corps of Engineers, seeking to prevent disastrous downstream flooding, urged the creation of dams across the Missouri River and its tributaries to control the release of spring runoff. He also suggested that navigation on the Missouri would be improved should his plan be implemented.[43]

Taking the arguments into consideration, Congress determined that an amalgamated plan of action should be adopted, and the Federal Flood Control Act of 1944 came into being. More popularly known as the Pick-Sloan Plan, the agenda called for the creation of six dams across the Missouri and its tributaries. Work commenced on the dam in October 1947, following the acquisition of some 155,000 acres of land from the Fort Berthold Reservation of the Three Affiliated Tribes. Tribes' members argued long and hard to prevent the building of the dam, or at least the building of the dam in the selected location. Built where intended, the dam and ensuing lake would take the very best farmland of the reservation, separate families and kinship groups, eliminate the collection of wild fruit and the cutting of fence posts for cash, and ultimately reduce the income of farming Indians to below 50 percent of its previous level.[44] Despite the Herculean efforts of tribal chairman George Gillette to produce a different end to the story, the Three Tribes' council signed the contract to sell their lands and improvements to the federal government for $5,105,625. A private appraisal later suggested that the tribes had been damaged to a total of $21,900,000. Congress ultimately boosted its compensation by $7,500,000, still some $9,000,000 short of the fair market value. Lieu lands suggested for the tribe did not meet with satisfaction, ultimately reducing the reservation to 426,413 acres, down from its original 12,500,000 acres in 1851.[45]

Before the dam's dedication on June 11, 1953, 349 households on the Fort Berthold Indian Reservation were uprooted, moved to new communities, separated from kinship groups, and isolated from traditional agricultural occupations. Rather than the numerous small communities that once filled the river bottom, Lake Sakakawea separated the formerly vibrant tribes into five distinct and isolated units. One tribal elder compared the impact of the dam on his community to that of the smallpox epidemics that ravaged the Mandan, Hidatsa, and Arikara in 1781 and 1837.[46]

When completed, Garrison Dam stood as the world's largest rolled-earth dam. Over 70,000,000 cubic yards of dirt went into the making of the dam, giving it a base a half-mile wide and a crest 60-feet wide, allowing for both rail and automobile traffic at the top. Lake Sakakawea, the reservoir created by the dam, has over 600 square miles of water surface and 1,500 miles of shoreline. It is the largest man-made body of water within the confines of a single state.[47]

Lake Sakakawea with Garrison Dam at the far left

© Chuck Haney

Dedicating the dam with a shovelful of dirt, President Dwight D. Eisenhower unknowingly collaborated in another milestone of North Dakota history: the coming of television. Although some parts of the nation had enjoyed regularly scheduled broadcasts beginning in the mid-1940s, KCBJ-TV of Minot went on the air in 1953, as did WDAY-TV of Fargo and KFYR-TV of Bismarck. WDAY-TV went "live" on June 1, 1953, enabling it sufficient practice time to record the president's shoveling, and ushering in a new age for North Dakota.[48] Such television stations and those that would quickly follow added a new dimension to the lives of North Dakotans. Rather than the radios they had listened to for the previous thirty years, television provided the visual cues of a national culture.

President Dwight Eisenhower with North Dakota Governor Norman Brunsdale at the closing of Garrison Dam

State Historical Society of North Dakota, Film Collections

Also changing the national culture, and adding valuable federal dollars to the state's economy was Eisenhower's Federal-Aid Highway Act of 1954, augmented by the National Defense Highway System Act of 1956. Constructing Interstates 29 and 94 brought some $77,000,000 to the state, as well as federal oversight of the roads' construction. In order that North Dakota's urban areas might be more readily evacuated, as well as other states' urban areas accommodated, in the case of a nuclear attack, the limited-access roads provided rapid lanes to transport the masses in emergency situations. The plan also decreed that of the interstate miles constructed, one of every five would be totally straight, allowing for their use as airstrips in times of war or other calamity. Other federal aid projects brought in additional funds for state and local highways.[49] Hard-surfaced roads virtually guaranteed that North Dakotans would travel further and further afield, exploring the state and nation in greater detail than ever before.

Fueling the automobiles and semi-trucks that traveled the new interstate highway system was gasoline distilled from the oil fields of North Dakota. On April 4, 1951, after decades of searching the western landscape, oil burbled to the surface of the Clarence Iverson farm near Tioga. The discovery of oil in western North Dakota set off a boom unlike any other ever seen in the state. Strangers and Dakotans alike rushed to the newly named Williston Basin. Tioga grew some 250 percent in three years, and Williston saw similar growth resulting in individuals sleeping in grain bins, garages, and assorted sheds. Schools crowded beyond their capacity and social services were stretched to the breaking point.[50]

Amerada Petroleum Corp's No. 2 in Beaver Lodge Field, in Williams County, 1954

Institute for Regional Studies, NDSU, Fargo, ND. Used with permission.

With dozens of companies drilling, within ten years of the discovery of oil, nearly 3,000 wells pumped oil to the surface. With some 110,000,000 barrels of oil produced within the first decade of operation, refineries soon followed, adding a new dimension to the North Dakota economy, and providing some young men lucrative jobs and a reason to make their homes in the state.[51]

The oil fields provided some solace to the perpetual problem of North Dakota's youth leaving the state in near-record numbers. Although youth had left the state before in large numbers, most notably in the 1920s and 1930s, state officials again took notice of the number of young men and women leaving. Bryce Streibel, one-time majority leader of the state House of Representatives, and later state senator, noted in his 1983 retrospective that North Dakota's young men and young women were always in demand due to their willingness to work, and work hard.[52]

Had Streibel examined the Census of 1950, he would have determined that some 360,000 individuals living outside the state claimed nativity to North Dakota. However, not only were the youth of North Dakota looking to economic opportunity in far-flung locations such as California, Washington, Colorado, and Minnesota, some simply sought the urban life that North Dakota's largest cities—Grand Forks, Fargo, Bismarck, Minot, and so on—offered. Jobs beckoned, as did the relative availability of social opportunities, the comforts of electrical service, and the esoteric "modern life." By 1950, 34 percent of North Dakotans lived in communities of 2,500 or larger. Indeed, throughout the 1950s, 38 of the state's 53 counties lost population, as did 66 percent of the towns and villages.[53] The trend once commenced has not yet concluded.

As startling as any youth staring into the distance, any dam, any air force base, or any mile of interstate highway came the dramatic shift of state politics. For years, the Republican Organizing Committee (ROC) had controlled the state's political structure. Democrats, always a loyal minority, for all purposes found themselves locked out of the political process, as did more liberal-minded Republicans. Remnants of the Non-Partisan League (NPL) with scarce exception cast their ballots along with their Republican neighbors. However, within the NPL fissures occurred, with the Old Guard still inclined toward the GOP and the Insurgents leaning more and more towards the Democratic Party.[54]

By no means did the split occur overnight. Indeed, it was many years in the making. As early as 1952, the NPL struggled to provide a unified appearance as its members variantly offered their support to Dwight D. Eisenhower for president or for Adlai Stevenson for the position. The Stevenson supporters considered the true meaning of the NPL to be found in support for labor, the Farmers' Union, and the Democratic Party, and cheerfully referred to themselves as the Insurgents. In opposition stood the Old Guard, anti-labor, anti-Farmers' Union, and stalwartly Republican. Longtime North Dakota Republican politicians Representative Usher Burdick and Senator William Langer managed to stay free of the fray by refusing to align with either faction of the party.[55] As *Time* magazine noted, "Wild Bill" Langer found himself in a less-than-desirable position. If he remained with the Republican Party, he undoubtedly would lose a considerable portion of his electoral base. However, should he join the Democratic-NPL, which was his normal pattern of voting, he would lose all seniority in the Senate. *Time* noted that Langer proved uncharacteristically quiet in the aftermath of the split.[56]

Senator William Langer

State Historical Society of North Dakota, A1798

In 1956, it appeared that the time had arrived for the final split to occur. In that year, the NPL, still technically a separate party, determined to align itself with the Democratic Party. With the Old Guard absent in protest, the remaining members of the NPL voted 173 to 3 for the realignment. By doing so, the Democratic Party now stood stronger than at any time in its North Dakota existence. Accordingly, the party put forth the most liberal platform of its existence as well, urging a $1.25 minimum wage, repeal of the Taft-Hartley Act, 100 percent parity for family farms, and a graduated land tax on holdings worth $20,000 or more.[57]

Party realignment did not initially prove politically rewarding, at least in terms of offices held. Republican gubernatorial candidate John E. Davis handily won office over Wallace E. Warner, although the margin of victory was somewhat less than previous Republican governors had enjoyed. On the national ticket, the Republicans still held sway as well, handing Dwight D. Eisenhower 62 percent of the vote and Adlai Stevenson, the Democratic candidate, 38 percent of the vote. If the Democratic-NPL could take any solace in the election, it came in the fact that Eisenhower had defeated Stevenson even more strikingly in the 1952 race, 71 percent to 28 percent.[58]

In 1958, however, the Democratic-NPL showed signs of electoral life. In that fall's general election Quentin Burdick, son of Usher Burdick, became the first United States Representative from North Dakota to sit on the Democratic side of the aisle, ever.[59] The death of longtime Republican Senator William Langer on November 8, 1959, forced a special election to fill his seat, and continued the dramatic shift in North Dakota politics in the forthcoming decade.

As the decade of the 1950s came to a close, the hallmarks of the next decade's turning points could be discerned. Federal dollars poured into the state, while its youth looked longingly at the distant cultural and economic opportunities provided by their small black-and-white televisions. Farm size increased as farms and farmers decreased. Oil was discovered in western North Dakota, and set the stage for a series of booms and busts in the coming years.

The horizon twinkled ever so mysteriously as the 1950s turned into the 1960s.

Representative Quentin Burdick

U.S. Senate Historical Office

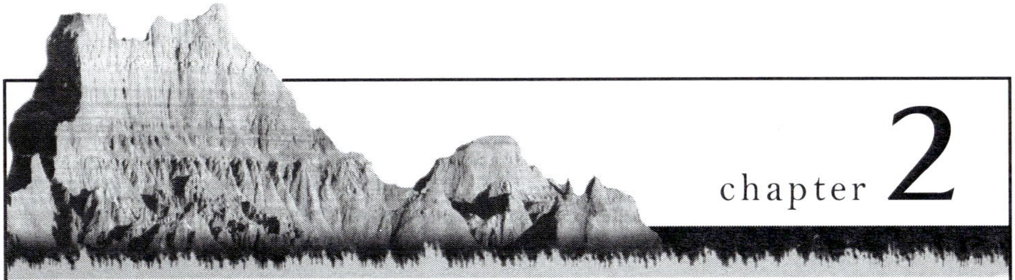

chapter 2

CHANGES
The Early 1960s

As the 1960s dawned, considerable change lay before residents of North Dakota. Before the midpoint of the decade, politics, the economy (particularly the agricultural sector), the role of the federal government, and popular culture would all undergo significant change, forcing North Dakotans to deeply consider their role not only in a national sense, but also in a global one.

The decennial census of 1960 showed a total of 632,446 individuals living in North Dakota as of April 1st of that year. While this represented an increase in population, a turnaround from the previous two censuses, the increase was not particularly substantial, a mere 2 percent. Natural increase, parents having children versus individuals moving into the state, would have produced an increase of approximately 15 percent, resulting in a population of 712,581.[60]

According to Elwyn Robinson, *History of North Dakota*, those individuals who left the state in pursuit of greater opportunities were often the ones the state most desperately needed to keep. They tended to be better educated, as well as in the height of their reproductive years, hence removing not only themselves from the state, but also their children, born and unborn. The result meant not only an ultimately declining population for the state, but also that by rearing and educating young men and young women, the state served only to subsidize the states to which they migrated.[61]

The elderly also left North Dakota, albeit in smaller numbers than their grandchildren. Upon retiring to Lodi, California, former Congressman Otto Krueger, who served in the United States House of Representatives from 1953 through 1959, remarked that because there were so many North Dakotans in California that it felt "just like home."[62]

Moreover, the statistics revealed a somewhat disquieting trend for those who treasured the image of North Dakota as a rural state, economically based upon agriculture. While without doubt the state's rural population still vastly outnumbered the individuals living in urban areas, the trend towards urbanization continued from the previous census. Now, some 35 percent of the state's residents lived in communities of 2,500 or more. In the census of 1950, a mere 27 percent of the population lived in urban areas. Not all of those living in rural areas, however, were farmers. By 1960, the farm population, as opposed to the rural population, had dropped to a mere 32 percent of the state's residents. In 1940, 51 percent of the state's residents lived on working farms. The pace towards urbanization was clearly speeding up.[63]

In addition, a pattern emerged as to where the vast majority of those leaving the land were coming from. Of the fourteen counties constituting the slope, that area between the Missouri River and the state's borders with Montana and South Dakota, eight lost at least 10 percent of their population. However, of the nineteen counties at least partially within 100 miles of the Red River, only six lost population of 10 percent or more and even those counties were at the western edge of the valley.[64]

Those counties gaining population were home to the state's largest cities: Fargo (Cass County), Grand Forks (Grand Forks County), Minot (Ward County), Bismarck (Burleigh County), Dickinson (Stark County), and Williston (Williams County). Clearly the state's largest cities beckoned with their greater social and economic opportunities. Sixty-six percent of the state's small towns lost population, as did 38 of the 53 counties. As a result of this eastern and urban migration, the number of viable towns declined, as did the number of schools, school districts, and churches, particularly in the western region of the state.[65]

Regardless of the continuing shift from rural pursuits to those of the urban environment, agriculture continued to be North Dakota's largest occupational category. Of the 153,523 men employed in the state in 1960, 52,106 claimed to be farmers or farm managers. Another 11,922 recorded themselves as farm laborers and farm foremen. While few of the 60,138 women employed in the state claimed agricultural pursuits as the primary source of their income, it is safe to assume that many farmers' wives, recorded only as "homemaker" on the census schedules, actually performed considerable farm labor throughout the year, even if without direct remuneration.[66]

As in previous decades, North Dakota's farmers and ranchers faced uncertainties; weather, crop prices, the increasing role of the federal government, and the implementation of new technologies all served to ensure the discontinuities of agricultural life. The decade started with two years of drought. Precipitation in both 1960 and 1961 fell

John F. Kennedy, William Guy, and Quentin Burdick (1960)

State Historical Society of North Dakota, 0763-01

considerably below the statewide average of 17.59 inches. In 1960, the statewide average fell to approximately 14.5 inches, with 1961's average falling to approximately 13 inches. Governor William L. Guy recalled that the drought of 1961 sidelined many of his plans for change during his initial year in office. Precipitation moderated by the mid-1960s to allow for more normal crop production, as well as grazing conditions.[67]

As had been the case for a number of years following the Korean War, the federal government continued its attempt to reduce surplus production and to increase prices. President John F. Kennedy supported mandatory production controls in order to maintain living standards for the nation's agriculturalists. Fraught with contention between members of the Democratic and Republican parties, as well as between members of North Dakota's predominant Farmers' Union and its lesser-supported Farm Bureau, Secretary of Agriculture Orville L. Freeman finally gained the authority to initiate a policy that allowed farmers who raised grain crops to reduce acreage and in return receive price supports for half their production in the form of negotiable certificates redeemable via the Commodity Credit Corporation (CCC). As prices rose, farmers could redeem these certificates for grain to sell on the open market. Most farmers, however, chose to have the CCC market their grain for them and accordingly received a check for their productivity.[68]

The power of new farming technologies frequently offset the federal government's goal of decreasing crop surpluses. In the aftermath of the 1930s Dust Bowl, more and more farmers throughout the United States had begun to practice soil conserving measures such as contour plowing, terracing, strip cropping, waterway reduction, and nurse-crop fallowing. While these moisture-preserving techniques added to the production of North Dakota's farmers, the application of new machinery and chemical inputs further elevated crop production.

By 1960, North Dakota farmers utilized more tractors and trucks per farm than any other state. The average farm had two tractors and one combine, up from one tractor and a fraction of a combine in 1945. From 1945 to 1963, the use of chemical fertilizers quadrupled in the state, while more and more farmers opted for certified seed rather than the planting of seed saved from the previous year's production. Purchased inputs rose by 60 percent and home-produced inputs fell by 35 percent over the same period. And, responding to government initiatives to reduce cropland under production, North Dakota farmers idled 30 percent of their crop acreage.[69]

Those with an eye on agriculture could note other changes on the farm front as well. From the onset of recordkeeping with regard to farm size in North Dakota, each report noted an increase in the acres under the production of individual farmers and ranchers while at the same time noting the decline in the actual number of farmers and ranchers. In 1945, 69,520 farmers tended farms of an average 590 acres. By 1950, 65,401 farmers did likewise for farms averaging 630 acres. By 1960, 54,928 farms existed in North Dakota with an average size of 755 acres. Undoubtedly new forms of technology, particularly tractors and combines made this expansion of acres possible.[70]

For those individuals remaining on the farm, life became somewhat easier over the early years of the decade. By the early 1960s, nearly every farm in the state was electrified and equipped with a telephone and a television, as well as running water, bathing facilities, and flush toilets. Many farm homes had acquired the major electrical appliances directed towards the homemaker: clothes dryers, refrigerators, freezers, washing machines, and the like.[71]

Despite these improvements and outward appearance of financial success, North Dakota farmers, and indeed those throughout the United States, did not prosper during the early years of the nation's seventh decade. The 32 percent of the state's residents who lived on farms claimed only 22 percent of the state's personal income. Low farm income led to low urban wages, leaving North Dakotans as a whole living on 78 percent of the national per capita income in 1960, $1,741 compared to $2,223.[72]

If farmers stayed relatively even in the first portion of the 1960s compared to their place throughout the postwar 1940s and 1950s, it came predominantly from increased production, not from higher crop prices. Indeed, an examination of prices for North Dakota's primary crops reveals a general downward trend. For example, in 1955, undifferentiated wheat sold for $1.98/bushel, for $1.74/bushel in 1960, and for $1.37/bushel in 1964. National average yield over this same period rose from 20 bushels per acre to 26 bushels to the acre. Durum wheat proved to be somewhat less profitable, selling for $2.43/bushel in 1955, $1.92/bushel in 1960, and $1.41/bushel in 1964. Yield per acre throughout the nation did, however, double from 14 bushels to the acre to slightly less than 28 bushels to the acre in 1965.[73]

Other crops showed a significant price decline from 1955 through 1960, only to rise slightly by the 1965 harvest. Corn, for example, sold for $1.35/bushel in 1955, $1.00/bushel in 1960, and $1.17/bushel in 1964. Production, however, rose from 42 bushels to the acre to nearly 63 over the same period. Soybeans, a relatively new crop for North Dakota's farmers and growing well only in the Red River Valley, sold for $2.22/bushel in 1955, dropping to $2.13/bushel in 1960, only to rise again to $2.62/bushel in 1964. Production rose from 20 bushels per acre to 23.[74]

Ranchers fared similarly over the course of the early 1960s. Fat steers, ranging from 1000 to1100 pounds, sold at Omaha in 1955 for an average of $22.40/cwt. In 1960 the price was $25.30/cwt., dropping to $22.34/cwt. by 1964. Returns for crops or beef are not adjusted for the rather low rate of inflation in the early 1960s, or for the increasing price of inputs.[75]

If the farm scene remained predominantly stable, albeit with a slight downward trend, the situation on North Dakota's political scene could scarcely have been considered normal, particularly from the Republican side of the ticket. A Democratic tide seemed to be rising, and precipitously so.

In the fall of 1958, Quentin Burdick became the first Democrat to serve North Dakota in the United States House of Representatives. In a tight race, with two seats open and four men contending, Burdick led the field. He surpassed the votes claimed by Republican Don L. Short by less than 2,000 ballots cast out of 368,437 cast. At the time, North Dakota had two seats in the lower chamber and candidates ran at large for the honor to serve.[76]

The death of long-term Senator William Langer on November 8, 1959, while in office, presented the opportunity to send a fresh face to Washington and Democrats most certainly hoped to capitalize upon the opening. Langer, having served essentially unopposed since 1941, had held government office of some sort since his election as Morton County States Attorney in 1914, and appeared to many to represent a time now passed in North Dakota's history. Democrats, Republicans, and Leaguers all looked covetously upon the open seat.

While the NPL had filed its candidates with the Democratic Party in the 1956 campaign, not all of its members could be declared confirmed to the decision. Indeed, in the spring of 1960, the NPL held a separate convention to discuss the various nominees, both Democratic and Republican, at the Patterson Hotel in Bismarck. Recalling the events some 30 years later, William Guy, the frontrunner for the Democratic nomination for governor, observed: "The furious debate and vociferous charges and counter charges reached a roaring pitch when Emmons County rancher Clarence Haggard leaped to the stage to try to hold the fort by keeping the young insurgents from taking the microphone. He brandished a neck yoke with a steel ring at each end. He swung the clanking neck yoke around his head as he shouted." In the ensuing melee, fists flayed and connected, pushes and shoves were exchanged, and at least some blood flowed. By the end of the evening, however, the NPL had joined the Democratic Party in support of its candidates, including Guy for governor and Quentin Burdick for United States Senator.[77]

To fill Langer's seat, the state called a special election for June 28, 1960, which also served as primary election day. Polling was brisk as Burdick faced sitting Governor John E. Davis for the right to represent North Dakota in the upper chamber. Not until two days later did the final count reveal Burdick as the winner. The margin of victory was only 1,118 out of 210,349 votes cast. Some pundits suggested that the success of Burdick foretold of a Democratic victory in the forthcoming presidential elections, while others perceived of his victory as a sign of farmers' disdain of Republican agricultural policies.[78]

In the election of 1952 Eisenhower had carried North Dakota by an astounding 70 percent, receiving 60 percent of the vote in his 1956 bid for reelection. Republicans generally felt North Dakota to be secure for the party, Democratic presidential candidates having carried the state on only four occasions.[79] Despite some suggestion that disgruntled farmers would cast their ballots for Democrat John F. Kennedy over Republican Richard M. Nixon, the GOP need not have feared. Although a comparatively close election, Nixon carried the state by a 30,000 vote margin, or 55 percent to Kennedy's 44 percent. For Guy, the picture was brighter. He defeated Republican contender C. P. Dahl by nearly 14,000 votes. North Dakota had become a two-party state.[80]

During his twelve years in office, Guy would build a reputation not only for modernizing the state's bureaucracy, but also for bringing valuable federal dollars to North Dakota. Indeed, at his initial election, Guy proclaimed his primary mission as gaining federal support for the first Rural Electric Cooperative (REC) in North Dakota and for the authorization and funding of the Garrison Diversion Project. His early backing of Kennedy ensured him the presidential ear and funds for the state.[81]

Even before Guy's election and inauguration, federal dollars continued flowing into the state for projects begun under the Eisenhower and Davis administrations. For example, construction on Garrison Dam, commenced in the 1940s, finally came to its conclusion. With its completion, western North Dakotans could count on less-expensive electric power as the dam's seven turbines produced approximately 515,000 kw per annum. Moreover, residents of Bismarck could be assured that the likelihood of springtime flooding had been drastically reduced. In addition to the practical matters of flood control and electric power generation, the dam's completion and the resultant reservoir—Lake Sakakawea—began to provide recreational opportunities for residents and tourists alike—boating, fishing, bird watching, camping, and so on.[82]

The construction of the federal interstate highway continued as well, and in the fall of 1960, Interstate 29, running north-south along the state's eastern edge finally made its way to the Canadian border. In doing so, North Dakota became the first state in the nation to connect with a similar highway system in a foreign land—Canada. Construction on Interstate 95 continued into the mid-1960s, reaching from Minnesota to Montana. By July 1, 1964, the federal government had spent nearly $102,000,000 in building the defense-oriented roadways, but could only claim to be slightly less than halfway done with the project through the state.[83]

On January 3, 1961, in one of his last acts as president, Dwight D. Eisenhower severed diplomatic ties with the island nation of Cuba citing its strengthening ties with the Soviet Union and its concomitant increasing threat to the United States. In April 1961, the Bay of Pigs debacle in which 1,500 anti-Castro Cubans were readied for attack upon their homeland, only to be met on the shores and brutally defeated in a matter of three days, deepened the distrust between the United States and Russia, as did the construction of the Berlin Wall, separating the eastern and western halves of that city.[84] Even more distressing was the discovery that Soviet premier Nikita Khrushchev had, in a display of brinksmanship, begun the installation of long-range missile sites in Cuba. The missiles, of course, could easily strike just about any mainland target in the United States. The resulting Cuban Missile Crisis of October 1962 brought the nation closer to nuclear engagement with the Soviet Union than at any point before or since. For a few moments it appeared that nuclear Armageddon was entirely a possibility. Accordingly, homeland defense assumed an even more vital appearance.

Although officially opened in 1957 with the arrival of the Air Defense Command 32nd Fighter Group, Minot Air Force Base assumed larger responsibilities as the Cold War threatened to once again turn hot. In January 1960, the 32nd Fighter Group brought the first F-106 Delta Dart to Minot, having arrived from a New York-based air force base to the more centrally located, and offensively structured, site. The scope of operations grew at Minot with the arrival of the 525th Bombardment Squadron to the 4136th Strategic Wing. Shortly thereafter, in July 1961, the first B-52H Stratofortress, named the "Peace Persuader," arrived on base. Five months later, the base received its first Hound Dog missile to give the B-52 "stand-off" capacity, or the ability to counterbalance the majority of the forces that might be targeted against it.[85]

In light of the world's precarious situation in 1961—most specifically the Bay of Pigs incident and the construction of the Berlin Wall—nuclear war with the Soviet Union appeared a distinct possibility. While Americans were encouraged to build fallout shelters and children practiced "duck and cover" routines at their school desks, the United States government determined to plant a field of missile silos in the heartland, most specifically in North Dakota.

The Air Force selected the land surrounding Minot Air Force Base for a new Minuteman I Intercontinental Ballistic Missile (ICBM) complex. To the Corps of Engineers Ballistic Missile Construction Office (CEBMCO) fell the responsibility of placing the 150 silos deemed necessary to the protect the United States, along with the ten launch complexes, all spreading over a 12,000-square mile area. Over 6,000 men and 1,100 pieces of equipment aided in the fulfillment of the $67.8 million contract, sans actual missiles.[86]

With the construction of the field locations commenced in early 1962, the Strategic Air Command activated the 455th Strategic Missile Wing in November 1962. Less than a year later, the first actual missile arrived in North Dakota courtesy of Hill Air Force Base in Utah. Within a matter of slightly over two years—April 1964—the 455th became combat ready. As the Minot Air Force Base official history notes: "The amber waves of grain over the North Dakota plains were implanted with a combat-ready ICBM system born of the latest American technology."[87]

By 1963, over 350 Minuteman missiles stood in their silos, tipped with nuclear warheads, fully armed and ready for deployment should the need arise. While all visitors from the Soviet Union were banned from the state of North Dakota, schoolchildren regularly took visits to their local silos, hearing time and again that should North Dakota become its own separate nation, it would have the third largest nuclear arsenal in the world, potentially making it the third most powerful nation in the world.[88]

Minot Air Force Base was not the only facility within the state to take the security of the United States seriously. Throughout the early portion of the 1960s, events at the Grand Forks Air Force Base took on new meaning and new urgency as war seemed to be on the horizon with the Soviet Union. Indeed, in February 1960, the Strategic Air Command organized the 905th Air Refueling Squadron at Grand Forks, with the first KC-135A Stratotanker arriving a scarce four months later. Earlier that same week, the Air Defense Command transferred the 18th Fighter-Interceptor Squadron and its F-0101B "Voodoos" from Wurtsmith Air Force Base, Michigan.[89]

Indeed, over the course of the early 1960s, more and more defensive operations transferred to Grand Forks Air Force Base from around the nation. Fighter wings and bombardment squadrons all came to the northern Great Plains, as did a combat support group. Perhaps more significantly, the air base also became the home of the 321st Strategic Missile Wing with its mission to oversee the deployment of the Minuteman II missile complex. The Strategic Missile Wing would not become operational until December 1966 with the actual completion of the missile field.[90] Elwyn B. Robinson, in *History of North Dakota*, estimated that each of the state's air force bases provided a yearly infusion of $200,000,000 into the local economy during the late 1950s and early 1960s.[91]

If such funding did not in and of itself give the state cause to celebrate, other infusions of cash undoubtedly did. Again, according to Robinson's estimations, the late 1950s and early 1960s saw federal dollars stream into North Dakota for the electrification of the state's rural regions ($119,000,000), for Garrison Dam ($294,000,000), and for interstate highways ($77,000,000). Investment dollars also came into the state, particularly as associated with the oil boom taking place in the western portion of North Dakota. Robinson estimated that private investors had infused some $650,000,000 to commence the boom, and aided in its continuation by an annual payroll of some $19,000,000.[92]

The Dakota Territory Centennial occurred in 1961, giving North Dakota residents something besides their plumping wallets to celebrate. In order to bestir tourism in the state, Governor Guy reaffirmed his predecessor's appointment of Marion Piper to coordinate a series of events to promote the state and its history. Guy and Piper, working with a team of citizen consultants, determined that since Theodore Roosevelt stood so prominently in the minds of many as a North Dakotan and as a hero for his role in the

Spanish-American War, as well as having made a significant contribution to the state's image as a western one, he might as well offer up the former president's image to a statewide award. Hence, the Rough Rider Award came into being to celebrate the successes of North Dakota residents. Named as the first Rough Rider recipient was Lawrence Welk, an entertainer personally known to the Guys, followed rapidly by Dorothy Stickney, actress; Ivan Dmitri, artist; Roger Maris, athlete; and Eric Sevareid, journalist.[93]

Lawrence Welk

The Welk Group, Inc./Santa Monica, CA.

Despite his success in bringing federal dollars to the state, or at least continuing those dollars instigated by his predecessor, life for Governor Guy had its difficulties. Not only did he have a near-drought to deal with, he also faced those individuals who believed that the election of a Democrat to the governorship had been a grievous error, regardless of his successes. With the majority of the state's daily newspapers arrayed against him, Guy took advantage of a regular opportunity to appear and to have his opinions voiced on the Farmers' Union *Focus on the News* television show. Fred Simonton, the program's "investigative reporter," provided the Democratic Party, Guy in particular, the chance to be heard when the majority of the news outlets in the state—radio, television, and press—could easily be declared Republican in orientation.[94]

The issues facing Governor Guy during his first term of office included, among other things, conditions at the state veteran's home in Lisbon and the state hospital for the mentally ill in Jamestown. Facilities and staffing at both institutions had clearly become inadequate for the demands being placed upon the structures. When the *Minot Daily News* suggested early in 1961 that Guy had been derelict in undertaking the repairs necessary for humane conditions to be the rule rather than the exception, he politely asked the paper's editor if he would care to serve as a concerned citizen and head up a committee to commence rectification of the difficulties.[95]

During his entire term of office, the resident population at Jamestown decreased from an approximate daily average of 1,700 in 1961 to an approximate daily average of

600 in 1971. Moreover, rather than simple custodial care, the hospital turned into an active treatment facility with modern kitchen facilities, a modern water treatment plant, specialized treatment for adolescents and children, as well as improved quantity and quality of staffing. Eight regional mental health clinics were built during the Guy years. In retrospect, Guy could declare that the improvement in children's care at the state hospital was one of his biggest accomplishments.[96]

Another significant accomplishment of Guy's first two administrations, 1961–63 and 1963–65, came in the form of a mandate dating from his predecessor's term of office. In 1959, the legislature passed an act based upon a 1957–58 legislative council to reorganize the government of the state of North Dakota into a more streamlined and efficient entity. Although technically to have begun before Guy's inauguration, no action had been taken well into his first term. Accordingly, Guy appointed Ralph Dewing to head the new Department of Accounts and Purchases. This department provided oversight to executive budget preparations, the review of claims against the state, payroll and accounting functions, as well as central data processing, printing, purchasing, and planning. Greater accountability, as well as better auditing of subdivisions of the state government resulted.[97]

Also of significance during the first years of Guy's governorship was the revitalization of the bank of North Dakota. A product of the Non-Partisan League's socialist platform of 1918–1919, the bank, over the course of the 1940s and 1950s, had fallen into a stagnant state of affairs. It no longer made farm loans and seemed to focus its attention on the purchase and sale of municipal bonds. According to Guy, the bank simply had no reason to get involved in anything different from its now-traditional trajectory. It was "safer" that way. However, "the people in the Industrial Commission felt that by leaving well enough alone, without trying to reactivate the bank of North Dakota, they could avoid some political consequences. At the same time the mood within the Republican party was that the state industries were really bad socialistic programs. Their mood was simply to let these socialistic industries die on the vine."[98]

Not willing to let the bank "die on the vine," Guy ordered an investigation to determine whether or not the bank was serving the purpose for which it was chartered. Finding considerable opposition in the Republican Party to the inquiry, as well as in T. W. Sette, the bank's manager, Guy pushed forward with a ten-point agenda geared towards awakening a "sleeping giant." While malfeasance could not be proven against Sette, clearly conflict of interest loomed perilously close to the horizon with the bank manager not only watching out for the state's interests, but also for his own as the owner of 17 percent the State bank of Burleigh County. Two interest-free accounts also came to light, one in New York City ($150,000) and the other in Duluth ($175,000). Sette ultimately resigned his position a year following Guy's inauguration.[99]

Guy saw the bank of North Dakota as a living being, able to adjust to the changing needs of the state. Accordingly, he sought the bank to create a secondary market for Federal Home Administration loans, to purchase economic development bonds, and to negotiate a reciprocal deposit policy with local banks. He also encouraged banks within the state to offer farmers low-interest loans via the Farmers Home Administration. This money would be developed at the bank over a five-year period, ultimately aiding the state's farmers and ranchers, yet covering the risk of locally owned banks.[100]

Not all economic development came on the farm front, or the banking front, during Guy's first years in office. Taking advantage of the apparent future need for additional energy resources, the Leland Olds Station Unit 1 electrical generating plant began construction in 1963. Consuming coal mined locally, the plant, when fully operational, was to use 3.3 million tons of lignite per year in its generation of 290,000 horsepower/669 megawatts, predominantly for use in northern portions of South Dakota.[101]

The Leland Olds Station did not prove to be the only effort at economic diversification and industrialization to take place during the early years of the decade. In 1960, the Melroe Manufacturing Company of Gwinner opened, manufacturing its Bobcat tractor-loader for dispersal throughout the Western world. The Dakota Salt and Chemical Company opened a plant near Williston the same year.[102] The state seemed to be moving forward under the guidance of the youthful, energetic Guy.

Of course, not everyone perceived that Guy served the state well, or for that matter that any Democrat could serve the interests of the state as well as any Republican. Accordingly, in the election of 1962, Guy faced exceptionally stiff competition in the form of Mark Andrews, a Mapleton farmer. Winning by a mere 2,007 votes, Guy retained his seat, only to see Andrews win a special election to finish out late Representative Hjalmar C. Nygaard's term. Republicans continued to hold all federal legislative positions, with the exception of Quentin Burdick as United States senator. All of the seats of the state cabinet were held by Republicans.[103]

In 1964, following a constitutional amendment to provide for a four-year term for the governor and other state officials rather than the previous two-year terms, Guy again stood for election. This time, he easily defeated the Democratic candidate Don Halcrow of Drayton by a comfortable margin. What was more unusual about the election, however, was the success of the Democratic ticket on the national level, as represented in North Dakota. Rather than marking their ballots for the Republican candidate out of sheer habit, the populace, potentially out of fear of the exceedingly right-wing Barry Goldwater, cast their ballots for Democrat Lyndon B. Johnson, 149,784 to 108,207.[104] By all accounts, the state had become one of two parties. The question remained to be seen if the Democrats had built a sufficient base to maintain their challenge.

chapter 3

DIFFICULT DAYS

The Latter 1960s

Although William L. Guy remained governor for the remainder of the 1960s, federal dollars continued to flow into the state and agriculture remained the primary occupation within North Dakota, the latter half of the 1960s presented the state with a series of challenges—political, economic, and cultural—that would provide a time of trial for the Flickertail State.

As 1965 dawned and both Lyndon Baines Johnson and Bill Guy took their oaths of office, the nation's population stood at 194,302,963 and that of North Dakota at 649,000, up some 17,000 individuals, nearly 3 percent, since the last enumeration. Many of those individuals newly counted in North Dakota could be attributed to the coming of the Minot and Grand Forks Air Force bases. The bases, once fully operational, provided at least 10,000 airmen for the count; their multiple dependents aided the population figures as well.[105]

While most of the state's residents still lived in rural areas, fewer and fewer considered themselves to be farmers. Many residents of rural areas had begun to commute to the state's small metropolitan areas in pursuit of a more regular paycheck, insurance benefits, and the expectation of fewer backbreaking hours in the field or on the range. Agricultural prices in comparison to inputs and consumables, a decade of inflation, albeit it mild in comparison to what would follow, a period of rather volatile weather and its resultant lower crop productivity hastened some from the farm, at least during the daylight hours.[106]

Over the course of the latter half of the 1960s, corn prices remained steady at $1.16/bushel, 1965 and 1969, albeit with slightly improved return on bushels per acre produced: 74 in 1965, compared to 85 in 1969. Wheat, North Dakota's cash crop, saw greater variability in prices received. In 1965, farmers could expect $1.35/bushel and in 1969, $1.25/bushel. Productivity climbed approximately four bushels to the acre in the latter half of the decade. Durum remained nearly steady throughout the 1965–69 period. At the onset it sold for $1.32/bushel and at the close $1.31/bushel. Productivity had increased by less than one bushel per acre. With regard to soybeans, in 1965, a farmer could expect approximately $2.54/bushel for his labor; in 1969, the return was somewhat less: $2.35/bushel. Productivity had risen by a scant three bushels to the acre.[107]

Ranchers could expect a somewhat better return on their labors, at least in terms of percentage. While beef sold for $25.06/cwt. in 1964, it sold for $29.68/cwt. in 1969.[108]

Of course, the inputs to the increased productivity did not come without cost. While prices paid for individual inputs varied from region to region, and are not readily accessible, it is fair to say that the cost of fertilizer, herbicides, pesticides, diesel fuel, gasoline, machinery, repairs, taxes, and the like did not decline over the course of the decade. Interestingly, more and more farmers took jobs off of the farm, presumptively to make ends come closer to meeting. One estimate has one-third of all 1965 farmers working off the farm at least 100 days or more per year. More and more farm wives also left the farm for a few hours per day, or perhaps a day or two per week for paid employment.[109]

As more and more of North Dakota's farmers found farm life to be less than satisfactory, for whatever reason—financial, social, intellectual or cultural—the number of active farms and ranches within the state declined, even as their sheer size rose. In 1965, for example, 49,500 farmers and ranchers tended to the state's 42,000,000 agricultural acres, resulting in an average operation of 848 acres. By 1969, however, only 46,000 farmers and ranchers remained on the land, meaning an average size of 911 acres per unit. It must, of course, be remembered that due to the size of North Dakota, as well as its climatological variances from east to west, farm size actually varied considerably from the Red River Valley to the Badlands. Moreover, not all community institutions could be maintained in light of the dwindling population. Schools, churches, small town businesses, and the like adapted, or disappeared.[110]

Weather rarely cooperates with the dreams of farmers and ranchers; the rain is too sparse or too much; the temperatures are too hot or too cold; the frost comes too early or too late. It is the farmer's constant lament; all he can do about the weather is complain. However, it can be freely said that North Dakota's farmers and ranchers of the latter half of the 1960s certainly had their fair share to complain about. With a statewide trend of some 17.6 inches of precipitation over the course of the year, 1966, 1967, and 1969 all fell below the average. Indeed, in 1967 a statewide average of only 14 inches of precipitation fell.[111]

Other years were challenging for their own reasons, not only for ranchers and farmers, but for urbanites as well. In 1965, for example, the Red River of the North overflowed its banks in mid-April following a particularly heavy rain on deeply frozen soil. Damage to the urban areas adjacent to the Red River totaled approximately $3 million. In total, costs to agricultural productivity, lost livestock, and lost rural dwellings and assorted structures ran to $14 million.[112]

A single year later, the Red River of the North again displayed its strength, as well as its capacity to inflict damage. An early March blizzard dropped more than two feet of snow throughout the eastern portion of North Dakota, forcing the construction of dikes in anticipation of high waters resulting from the thaw. Although only half a foot higher at the crest than the prior year, 44.9 versus 45.6 feet, the experience was considerably more expensive. Extra time to prepare for the potential of flooding led to the construction of significantly higher dikes with concomitant expense. The estimate for flood preparations and damage in the Grand Forks region alone totaled slightly over $4 million.[113]

The blizzard that precipitated the Red River flood of 1966 was, in and of itself, the stuff of legends. Commencing on March 2 and lasting through March 5, a blizzard dumped more than two feet of snow across the Dakotas, northern Minnesota, and southern Manitoba. With winds at gale force—some estimates have the wind blowing at 70 miles per hour—drifts piled up thirty feet or more, closing rural roads as well as interstates, shutting down all rail transportation, and isolating individuals throughout the region.[114]

The storm's severity stopped the Northern Pacific Railway's "The North Coast Limited" near Glen Ullin. Stranded for several days, the train soon used its store of food, and had to rely upon the kindness of the community to help feed its 131 passengers and crew. The Great Northern chose not to run trains during the height of the blizzard and for several days thereafter.[115]

At least five individuals perished during the storm, including two young girls. Carleen Welk, the six-year-old daughter of Mr. and Mrs. Eugene Welk, became separated from her older brothers after they had left the safety of their home to take care of livestock. Little Carleen was with her brothers at the chicken coop, but between the coop and the barn, she disappeared. The boys and their father looked for her as best they could in the howling wind and blowing snow. They checked each of the outbuildings—the coop, the barn, the granary, and a second barn—all without success. Then on Saturday, two days after she left the warmth of her home, Carleen's body was discovered. Lacking other resources, her father placed his daughter's frozen body in a granary. A helicopter from the Minot Air Force Base carried Carleen's body from her home to the local mortuary.[116]

Twelve-year-old Betty Deede, daughter of Mr. and Mrs. Raymond Deede, Woodworth, also perished in the storm. Leaving the comfort of her home to shut the door to the chicken coop, Betty made her way to the barn where her nephew had decided to wait out the storm. Betty then determined to return to her home, some 200 feet away, but became disoriented. Searchers found her body the following morning, a half mile from her home, lying in an open field.[117] Livestock by the thousands perished.

Mother Nature also struck out at Minot. Situated just below where the Mouse and Des Lacs rivers join, Minot has been susceptible to flooding throughout its existence. The flood of April 1969 came not only from the flooding of the aforementioned rivers, but also from the melting of deep snows, which had blanketed the region throughout the winter. When the waters of the Mouse met with those of the local melt, flooding was all but guaranteed. Accordingly, on Easter Sunday, April 6, diking started in Minot, aided by the men of the Minot Air Force Base. By mid-week, over 300 homes had been evacuated by thousands of volunteers, while others labored to build dikes of clay and sandbags. An estimated 15,000 individuals worked to save the city, its residents, and their possessions. Twelve thousand individuals, forced from their homes, took shelter with friends and family, as well as at local schools. Before the Mouse again flowed between its banks on May 15, an estimated $10 million in damages had been incurred.[118]

Farmers, the single largest occupational group in North Dakota, felt the force of nature worse than any other group. The struggle to plant, to harvest, to keep livestock fed and watered, and to make a living in the cost/price squeeze drove some 10,000 farmers from the land during the course of the 1960s.[119] Opportunities awaited farmers, and others, in newly operational industrial concerns.

The Leland Olds Station Unit 1 of Basin Electric Cooperative, commenced in 1963, went online in January 1966. Named for the former Federal Power Commission chairman, when the station began operations, it was the single largest lignite-based power plant in the entirety of the Western Hemisphere and had cost a total of $36 million to construct. Soon other electrical generating facilities commenced construction, including Leland Olds Station Unit 2, which, when completed in 1975, could produce 590,000 horsepower of energy. Inflation and generating capacity took their toll; the second plant required $109 million to become operational. The plants clustered around Lake Sakakawea and Garrison Dam where plentiful water aided in the process of producing electricity. At the close of the 1960s, no state produced as much electrical energy at the mine mouth from coal as did North Dakota.[120]

Oil provided another avenue of employment, as well as energy production. During their first decade of production, 1951–61, the western oil fields produced some 110,000,000 barrels of oil and with its accompanying natural gas, generated approximately $280,000,000 in revenue for investors. The boom continued into the latter 1960s, albeit without the fervor of the 1950s and early 1960s. The drilling peak for North Dakota came in 1966 when 1,965 active wells produced 27,000,000 barrels of oil over the course of the year.[121]

In 1920, the Rosses—grandfather John, son Ferdinand, and grandson Walter—planted 10 acres of sugar beets. They were not the first to do so, but did represent the first effort at commercial production of sugar beets. They sold their entire crop to Minnesota Sugar, having to ship the beets to Chaska, Minnesota, for processing. By 1925, representatives of American Beet Sugar Company, later American Crystal Sugar Company, ventured that a processing plant in the valley might prove profitable for all involved, including the growing number of North Dakota farmers raising their first crops of beets. According a plant came to fruition in East Grand Forks, Minnesota. It processed its first harvest in 1926.[122]

In 1948, a processing plant opened at the southern end of the valley. The Moorhead, Minnesota, plant operated by American Crystal meant to cash in on the increasing production of sugar beets, bestirred by wartime exigencies. Crookston, Minnesota, opened its American Crystal processing plant in 1954, to relieve some of the burden carried by the aging East Grand Forks plant.[123]

Despite the growth of sugar beets in Pembina, Walsh, Grand Forks, Steele, Traill, Cass, and Richland counties in North Dakota, however, no plant existed within the state for the processing of the increasingly lucrative crop. In Drayton, the lack of processing facilities encouraged a group of businessmen to form the Drayton Economic Development Council with the goal of attracting and building an agricultural base for the community. Following a series of telephone calls, letters, and personal visits, former Secretary of Agriculture Charles Brannan became an interested bystander. Brannan who had previously worked with American Crystal to arrange beet processing plants seemed to augur well for the development council. By the autumn of 1961, a feasibility plan was drawn up and sent to interested parties: the United States Department of Agriculture, American Crystal, valley sugar beet growers, and potential investors. The federal government agreed to an allotment for the beet growers and the plan hastened forward. By the autumn of 1965, the Drayton plant began to process sugar beets from the northern end of the valley.[124]

Not all good news for farmers came from American Crystal and the United States Department of Agriculture. Some came from the Congress of the United States and the pen of President Lyndon Baines Johnson. The story behind Johnson's signature dated from the Pick-Sloan Plan, which produced Garrison Dam as well as Fort Peck Dam in Montana. Initially, members of the Bureau of Reclamation felt that water from the dams could be used to irrigate approximately one million acres of land to the north and west of Lake Sakakawea from the reservoir. However, they soon discovered that the soil between Crosby and Mohall was of unusual density and would not profit from irrigation. The plan was temporarily shelved.[125]

Although it took its time in doing so, the Bureau of Reclamation did, indeed, produce a second plan to irrigate acres and acres of North Dakota. The land selected for irrigation lay in the east-central region of the state and by most measures did not require irrigation, at least not to the extent that the previously identified acres needed it. However, in 1957, the bureau unveiled its plan. Calling for 6,773 miles of main and lateral canals, eight reservoirs, 656 pumping stations and 9,300 miles of drains, the newly named Garrison Diversion would pump millions of gallons of water annually to the Devils Lake region and to points further south and east. The bureau estimated that completing the project would take at least 60 years and cost an estimated $529,000,000. Quick calculations revealed that the total value of North Dakota's farmland in 1954 stood at a mere $1.5 billion. As an aside, some three million acres of North Dakota farm ground remained out of production due to federal programs to reduce agricultural output.[126]

Few outside the state could find any good reason for the construction of the Garrison Diversion, except as pure political pork. Yet North Dakotans pushed on, forming the 28-county Garrison Diversion Conservancy and gaining state legislative authorization for a tenth of a mill on all real and personal property within the confines of the district, generating approximately $34,000/year to continue the fight for federal support, as well as to continue organizational work within the conservancy district.[127]

Despite considerable native support for the plan, regardless of the cost, federal authorization did not come regardless of its presentation before the Congress in 1960, 1963, and 1964. Even when a reduced plan was offered—a mere $183,000,000—federal approval was not forthcoming. The plan again reached Congress again in 1965, passing both houses of the legislature and landing on the president's desk. While he signed the authorization on August 5, 1965, the point was essentially moot for those interested in irrigating North Dakota. Congress had appropriated *no* funds for the construction of the project.[128]

With limited funds later made available, as well as with a one mill tax on real and personal property within the conservancy district, initial labor began on the diversion in 1968 with the Snake Creek pumping plant. Work on the plant, intended to lift Missouri River water from Lake Sakakawea to the McClusky Canal, continued until 1976 at a cost of $19.2 million. The McClusky Canal, meant to move water from the Missouri River to the central portion of the state and to stretch some 74 miles from Lake Audubon to the headwaters of the Sheyenne River, commenced construction in 1969, also coming to completion in 1976.[129] Economists and environmentalists have prevented the completion of the diversion system ever since.

McClusky Canal Headworks

Photograph courtesy of the U. S. Geological Survey

If the federal government was loathe to pour too much money into the Garrison Diversion, that was not the case with the United States military, particularly the United States Air Force. Throughout the latter part of the 1960s, despite the nation's involvement in the Vietnam War, North Dakotans' attention remained riveted upon the possibility of a Soviet nuclear attack. Accordingly, missiles; silos; Minutemen I, II, and III; interceptors, antiballistic missile systems; Sentinels; and Safeguards became part of the common lexicon.

When the Soviets and Americans determined that mutually assured destruction did not necessarily bode well as a foreign policy, the determination was made to allow each nation to construct an antiballistic missile defense system. And although President Richard Nixon argued that it should be located in the eastern portion of the United States, many residents of the seaboard did not welcome the opportunity to have a nuclear missile silo in their backyard. North Dakotans, however, welcomed the opportunity with open arms. The contract to construct the defensive structure to protect 150 of the nation's Minuteman II missiles and their launch center in Grand Forks totaled some $5.7 billion. Nekoma, in Cavalier County, was designated home to the tall pyramid-shaped Missile Site Radar centers, designed to track incoming warheads and to guide the interceptors to their assigned targets. Given the four-sided structure, the sky could be watched in all directions up to 300 miles distant. Additional radar sites allowed airmen to scan the skies for incoming missiles to a distance of 800 miles. In addition, the Nekoma site itself required a defensive structure. Underground, and nearby, sat the launchers for thirty Spartan and sixteen Sprint nuclear-tipped weapons. Four remote and unnamed sites hosted another fifty or so Sprint missiles. Funded in 1969, actual construction on the missile silos commenced in 1970.[130]

Stanley R. Mickelsen Safeguard Complex, Nekoma

Photo by David Novak, srmsc.org.

While some argued that the missile defense system could only be considered a boondoggle of massive proportions, including United States Senators George McGovern and Henry Jackson, others welcomed the federal dollars to the state. Nekoma, Langdon, and Cavalier all blossomed as the massive construction project brought business to the small communities. Dreaming of a bright future and a long Cold War, the towns indebted themselves for sewers, schools, and water and street facilities.[131] For some, North Dakotans in particular, the Cold War did not seem all that bad, nor did the Vietnam War.

Despite the ongoing Vietnam War, and the state's reputation for isolationist sentiment, little protest erupted around the distant Asian war. Governor Guy urged de-escalation of the war and when called upon by President Johnson went to Vietnam personally to oversee the first free presidential elections in that nation in 1972.[132]

Guy remained a popular figure in North Dakota. In 1962, North Dakota voters approved a constitutional amendment changing the term of office for most elected officials to that of four years. Accordingly with his success in the 1964 campaign, Guy became the first governor to serve a four-year term, meaning he did not stand for election until 1968. His opponent that year in the general election was a Bismarck car-dealing millionaire: Robert McCarney. Over the years, McCarney had earned a reputation as "the fourth branch of government." Others commented less charitably that the hazards of living in North Dakota were blizzards, mosquitoes, and Robert McCarney.[133]

North Dakota's constitution allows for the easy placement of initiative, referendum, and recall on the ballot. Indeed, over the years, it has become increasingly easy for individuals to challenge legislation, to propose legislation, or to dismiss elected officials. As part of its proud progressive heritage, North Dakotans can also amend their constitution via a petition procedure. Over the years, North Dakotans have voted to keep the products of the Non-Partisan League in place, to prohibit corporate farming, to permit movie theaters to be open on Sunday afternoons, and to ban parking meters in most instances.[134]

Actively involved in the political scene since 1963, McCarney had managed via the referendum to overturn a tax package that would have raised income, as well as other, taxes in the state. By a margin of six to one, North Dakotans supported his measure. In 1965, he managed to cancel another tax package, this time by a margin of four to one. Overall, he had proven to be one of Governor Guy's thorniest constituents, stymieing a series of proposals that needed state tax dollars to function. Challenging the endorsed Republican candidate and squeaking by on less than 5,000 votes, McCarney took his case for fiscal conservatism to the people. On November 5, 1968, however, Guy again prevailed, defeating the car dealer 135,955 to 108,382. Regardless of the strength displayed by Guy, the electorate returned a solid Republican cabinet. The entire congressional delegation, except Senator Quentin Burdick, fell into the Republican column as well.[135]

If Republicans feared that the presidential election of 1964 portended ill for the party in North Dakota, they need not have worried. In 1964, the state had swung decidedly in favor of Democrat Lyndon B. Johnson over Republican Barry Goldwater; in 1968, the trend reversed when Republican Richard Nixon soundly trounced Democrat Hubert Humphrey in the presidential contest, 138,669 to 94,769. Despite his personal popularity, Governor Guy could not hand the Minnesotan North Dakota's four electoral votes.[136]

For those with sharp eyes, changes loomed on the horizon. In 1967 when the United States Bureau of the Census revealed its annual estimate of the state's population, it trended downward—dramatically. In 1966, the Bureau had estimated a population of 647,000. In 1967, however, the estimate fell to 626,000, a loss of over 21,000 individuals in a single year.[137] The Bureau did not suggest causation; however, an exploration of North Dakota in the latter 1960s does suggest a reason or two for the dramatic change in population. First, the oil boom of the 1950s did not continue into the 1960s. Indeed, the middle of the decade saw prices for crude oil drop throughout the world, leaving the more isolated wells of western North Dakota to bear a greater portion of the burden of the presumed excess. Ultimately, the young men who had come to Williston, Tioga, and other parts of Williams County at the height of the boom left, taking their families with them.[138]

Dramatic changes also took place on the farm during the closing years of the 1960s. With the increasing use of mechanical and chemical inputs into the process of producing a crop, expenses associated with farming skyrocketed; prices did not. Many farmers operated on only the slimmest edge of profitability. While some farmers chose to get larger and larger over the course of the decade, others made the decision that the vagaries of farm life were not for them and headed to the urban centers of North Dakota, if not to places outside the state. From 1960 to 1969, the number of farms in North Dakota dropped from 56,000 to 46,000, while their acreage expanded by 160 acres, on average.[139]

Additionally, the latter 1960s produced a restless culture as individuals sought self-actualization through whatever means possible. For some this meant leaving agriculture for industrial pursuits, or perhaps even leaving the state, but for others, particularly the youth of the state, it meant expressing themselves in ways unknown to their parents. Dramatic changes in clothing, music, political activism, sexual mores, drug use, and hair styles affected the nation during the rather turbulent 1960s, and North Dakota did not escape the challenges.

Of particular note regarding the challenges to traditional social values was the "Zip to Zap." The zip began quite innocently in the late spring of 1969. Chuck Stroup, a North

Dakota State University student with time on his hands but no cash in his pockets, decided that he and his pals would head to Zap, North Dakota, population 271, for a weekend during spring break. Advertising in the NDSU student paper—*The Spectrum*—publicized the gathering throughout not only North Dakota, but the entire Midwest. Stroup's "Grand Festival of Light and Love" captured the attention of the region's youth as nothing had before.[140]

Taking place several months before the more infamous Woodstock, the Zip expanded exponentially in the minds of state and local officials from the simple fun of students on break to a more politically charged event. Nationally, National Guard troops had been called out over 200 times to quell student unrest on issues related to the Vietnam War, civil rights, and the simple clash of cultures resulting from generational change. A certain fear filled the air, but the initial intent clearly did not have significant political undertones. Students simply wanted to have fun.[141]

Residents of Zap, for the most part, saw the potential invasion of students as a chance to make money. Some rented their pastures for campers; others hired local bands for entertainment. The café started to develop "Zapburgers" and the local bars determined to lay in an extra stock of beer. Not knowing what to expect, Governor Guy visited with the State Highway Patrol to control potential traffic jams; he also took the time to visit with the National Guard should the community and the students somehow lose control of the event.[142]

By early evening Friday, May 9, 1969, students began to descend upon Zap. Before long, the beer ran low and the bar owners, determining to make the best of a bad situation, raised the prices on the remaining stock. The café closed due to lack of supplies and the students grew unruly. Some vomited in public; others urinated. As the temperatures dropped, students located materials from a building undergoing demolition to start a bonfire. Some residents of Zap attempted to reason with the students, asking them to go home; remarkably, a goodly number did, but others did not. In essence, the remaining students started to riot, breaking into the café and one of the bars, trashing them in the process.[143]

Guy called in 500 National Guardsmen, and by dawn they ringed the town. Although a mere 200 of the youth remained awake and going strong, the Guardsmen moved in and quelled the ongoing riot. Guardsmen also awakened some one thousand students who had fallen asleep, taking comfort in whatever shelter, pasture, or automobile they could find. Hungry, hungover, and cold, the students dispersed with only the slightest of resistance. The story did, however, make the CBS evening news, *Stars and Stripes*, and the Soviet Union's *Pravda*, providing little-desired publicity for the state. Damages to the community were estimated at $25,000, and the bills were sent to the student bodies at the University of North Dakota and North Dakota State University. They paid the bills.

Although rowdy beyond the conservative state's usual demeanor, the Zip to Zap portended the changes taking place not only in North Dakota, but also in the United States. As the 1960s turned to the 1970s, the state and its residents would be forced to deal with antiwar protests, civil rights movements, feminist charges, agricultural decline, and the out migration of over half of its youth.

chapter 4

THE BEST OF TIMES AND THE WORST

The Early 1970s

To paraphrase a somewhat better known author, depending upon one's perspective, North Dakota in the early 1970s could be considered both the best of times and the worst of times. At the onset of the decade, the Williston region oil boom collapsed, turning once prosperous towns of the 1960s into mere shadows of their former selves. However, the agricultural sector of the state prospered in the early portion of the decade, bringing wealth to farmers not experienced since the heady days of World War II. Elsewhere, federal dollars continued to trickle in to continue labor on the Garrison Diversion and McClusky Canal, as did funding for missiles, airplanes, airmen, and silos to defend against the potential of a Soviet attack. Other segments of the economy varied, as did the weather, the politics of the era, and the social climate.

The first hint that affairs of the Flickertail State stood in flux came with the official release of the 1970 census. According to that document, the population of North Dakota fell precipitously over the latter portion of the 1960s. While the United States Bureau of the Census recorded 632,446 individuals living in North Dakota on April 1, 1960, it could find only 617,761 on that date in 1970.[145] For those not so nimble with their mathematical skills, that marked a 2.3 percent decrease over the previous decade.

Moreover, population did not drop evenly over the entire state. A comparison of rural and urban illustrated that while the state's rural population still predominated, 56 percent rural to 44 percent urban, the movement towards towns and cities, as well as to other states, continued to rise relatively unabated.[146]

The largest drop in population came in the western counties. For example, of the 14 counties composing the slope, only one showed growth. Stark County, home to Dickinson, grew by a mere 6.3 percent over the decade. Conversely, Dunn, Slope, and Billings counties lost, respectively, 22.9, 21.6, and 20.9 percent of their population over the decade. Most other counties in the region lost at least 10 percent of their population throughout the 1960s. Sioux County, home of a portion of the Standing Rock Indian Reservation, lost a mere .8 percent of its population, bucking the general trend of the region.[147]

To find areas of growth, one needed to look to the eastern portion of North Dakota, particularly to the more urban areas already in existence. For example, Grand Forks County, home of Grand Forks, the University of North Dakota, and the Grand Forks Air Force Base, grew nearly 26 percent, and Cass County, home of North Dakota State University and the state's industrial center, grew 10 percent. Other gaining counties for the 1960s included Burleigh County, home of the state capital; Ward County, home to Minot, the Minot Air Force Base, and a state university; Rolette, home of the Turtle Mountain Indian Reservation; and, as previously mentioned, Stark County, home to Dickinson and its state university.[148]

The population of North Dakota included 14,369 individuals of Native American descent, undifferentiated. This marked an increase of 2,633 individuals from the census of 1960. The Indian population of North Dakota could only be described as rural because 87 percent of the state's Native Americans lived in areas of less than 2,500 individuals.[149]

Clearly, the majority of the state's counties and communities lost population over the course of the decade. Interestingly enough, several counties lost population overall, but illustrated a slight growth in their urban centers. Barnes, Benson, Bottineau, Morton, Ramsey, Richland, Stutsman, and Walsh counties recorded an overall loss of population, but did see slight increases in their urban populations in comparison to their rural losses.[150]

Changes, not reserved for North Dakota alone, visited the American countryside. Although the nation as a whole grew from 179,323,175 to 203,235,298, an increase of slightly over 13 percent, its rural population dropped from 30.1 percent to 26.4 percent, or by nearly a half million individuals in raw numbers from 1960 to 1970.[151]

With regard to agriculture in North Dakota, the number of farms dropped significantly over the course of the 1960s. In 1960, North Dakota had approximately 56,000 farms, averaging 751 acres each. By 1970, however, the number of farms in North Dakota dropped to approximately 45,500, with an average farm size of 921 acres. Considering that farms in the eastern portion of the state recorded fewer acres than the ranches of the western portion of the state, the numbers are, of course, somewhat skewed, but the fact of the matter is that the number of farmers/ranchers needed in North Dakota dropped over the course of the 1960s, forcing many to leave the land for variant, urban occupations. As R. Douglas Hurt notes in *American Agriculture: A Brief History*, increased irrigation; improved herbicides, insecticides, and fertilizers; and their increased use, as well as improved and increased use of agricultural equipment, all served to make farmers more productive over the 1960s and into the 1970s. In the process, however, fewer farmers and ranchers were needed to feed the nation and maintain a healthy export market.[152]

Farm and ranch size continued to grow over the early 1970s. By 1974, the average operation in North Dakota stood at slightly over 969 acres. Between 1970 and 1974, 2,500 farmers left the land for alternate employment. Those that remained on the farm, however, did well for themselves and their families. In 1972, the United States brokered massive grain sales to the Soviet Union and Communist China, staving off not only famine in those regions of the world, but also improving relations with those nations, a factor that would come into play with reduced military tensions and the arsenals of the Great Plains. More directly apparent, however, was the incredibly enhanced prices that

North Dakota, and American farmers in general... received for their grain. In 1969, undifferentiated wheat sold in the United States for approximately $1.25/bushel. Production ran at slightly over 30 bushels to the acre. By 1974, undifferentiated wheat sold for an average of $4.09/bushel, albeit dry weather on the plains dropped production to approximately 27 bushels to the acre. Obviously, the price received more than made up for the reduced production.[153] Durum, the primary wheat used in the production of pasta products, sold for $1.31/bushel in 1969, yielding approximately 32 bushels to the acre. However, in 1974, durum sold for $5.96/bushel, despite the limitations imposed by relatively dry conditions and a limited harvest of 20 bushels to the acre.[154]

Although never a primary crop in North Dakota, the price farmers received for corn also rose in the early 1970s. In 1969, farmers received an average of $1.16/bushel for their corn; in 1974, the price received topped $3.00/bushel for the first time in American history. Farmers received an average of $3.02/bushel that year for their corn crop, despite the somewhat lessened harvest.[155] Soybeans, still not the most popular crop in North Dakota, also returned handsome profits for those willing to take a chance on planting them. In 1969, beans sold for an average of $2.35/bushel. In 1974, the price crossed the $6.00/bushel mark for the first time. Indeed, farmers received an average of $6.64/bushel for their beans that year. Once again, a somewhat reduced harvest had been compensated for by dramatically improved prices.[156]

Sugar beet growers in the Red River Valley enjoyed a number of profitable years in the early 1970s, the area less affected by the dry weather than other regions of the state, and the only portion of the state suitable for sugar beet production. Profitability, as well as conflict with existing entities, brought farmers together into the Red River Valley Cooperative, which ultimately brought a new sugar beet processing plant to the state. At Hillsboro, the cooperative turned its first beets into sugar in 1974.[157]

Crystal Sugar Refinery, Hillsboro, North Dakota

Courtesy, American Crystal Sugar Company.

Improved prices also brought benefits to ranchers during the early portion of the 1970s. Although not exported to either the Soviets or the Chinese in any substantial quantity, beef prices rose dramatically. While beef had sold for $29.68/cwt. in 1969, the 1974 market provided $41.89/cwt. for prime steers.[158]

Increasingly, farmers found themselves in the position to expand their holdings. As the foreign market gave every appearance of providing a constant outlet for excess domestic production, farmers sought loans to add to their land holdings, often willingly signing mortgages that just a few years prior they would have deemed excessive. Yet, the federal government, as it had in the aftermath of World War I, encouraged the nation's farmers, as Secretary of Agriculture Earl Butz once famously said, "to get big or get out" of agriculture. With the increasing indebtedness of farmers across the nation, not just in North Dakota, and at incredibly low rates of interest, the stage was set for disaster.[159]

Adding to the potential for disaster, the price of North Dakota farmland rose dramatically in the early 1970s. Slope grazing ground that sold for $101/acre in 1973 sold for $151 in 1974, having sold for only $72/acre in 1970. Cropland saw similar increases in sales value. In the northern Red River Valley, cropland that sold for $180/acre in 1970 increased to $395/acre just four years later. The same could be said for the majority of land throughout the state; a 41 percent increase in value was average. Prices rose dramatically on the vague promise that agricultural prices would remain high and consistent profitability would return to the farm and ranch front.[160]

On July 27, 1970, the State Mill and Elevator, a product of the state's 1910s flirtation with socialism and a boon to the state's agriculturalists, suffered a devastating fire. An estimated $5 million in damages occurred when flames broke out in the spring wheat and durum milling units. Beyond destroying the majority of the milling equipment, the structures of the mill incurred significant damage. Despite the expense, much of which was covered by insurance, no one gave real consideration to closing the mill and elevator. Indeed, the opportunity to revitalize the equipment and operations seemed too good to pass up. When Governor Guy officially rededicated the mill on January 31, 1972, the mill's capacity had been increased by 25 percent. At its rededication, the mill became one of the most modern facilities in the nation.[161]

If agriculture for the most part boomed in the early 1970s, the oil industry did not. Indeed, after an initial decade and a half oil rush, the international price of oil, as well as the expense of drilling for North Dakota's deeply seated basins, discouraged continued exploration and exploitation. Towns such as Tioga and Williston, which had once bustled with oil field activity and its ensuing calls upon housing, social services, schools, and the like, found themselves faced with an overbuilt infrastructure as the 1970s dawned. From 1950 to 1960, the population of Williams County rose from 16,442 to 22,051, having remained stagnant the previous decade. However, from 1960 to 1970, the population fell by some 3,000 individuals. Tioga rose from a population of 456 in 1950 to 2,087 in 1960, and back down to 1,667 by 1970. Williston witnessed similar swings in population, rising from 7,378 in 1950, to 11,866 in 1960, and back down to 11,280 in 1970.[162] International events would soon restore western North Dakota's oil fields to some of their prior glory.

As the economy of North Dakota as well as the rest of the nation changed, and population shifts occurred, it became clear that North Dakota would be losing one of its delegates in the United States House of Representatives. From 1913 through 1933, the state had three federal representatives, but following the census of 1930 suffered reapportionment and the loss of a representative. Now, it appeared that North Dakota would once again lose a representative. Indeed, as other regions of the nation grew, North Dakotans felt the sad truth of their declining population. Following the election of 1972, only one individual would represent the state in Washington, D.C. Two senators, as guaranteed by the United States Constitution, irrelevant of state population, would continue to represent the state in Congress. Given that three federal representatives once graced the halls of Congress on behalf of North Dakota, the reduction to a single representative came as somewhat of a blow to the state's pride.[163]

The loss of a representative did not consume the entirety of the state's attention with regard to politics in the early years of the decade. For years, individuals had dealt with changes in the state's initial constitution on a piecemeal fashion. Amended and restructured on occasion, the constitution appeared to many to be rather unwieldy. Encouraged by Governor William L. Guy, as well as a host of other individuals, the 41st Legislative Assembly, meeting in March 1969, determined to see if North Dakotans felt the same as their leaders. Accordingly, North Dakota House passed concurrent legislation with the Senate to place the call for a constitutional convention on the September 1970 primary election ballot. The measure handily passed the House, 72–19, and sailed through the Senate without opposition. On September 2, 1970, the citizenry of North Dakota approved the measure by a vote of 56,734 to 40,094.[164]

A nominating committee, composed of the governor, lieutenant governor, and attorney general, made a series of suggestions as to potential conventioneers. In accordance with the enabling legislation, a total of 98 individuals would oversee the process. Along with the 98 recommended by the governor's group, citizens put forth the names of another 141 individuals. In the general election of November 1970, the electorate picked the delegates charged with restructuring the state's constitution. Representing all corners of the state, a wide variety of professions were represented: farmer, housewife, mortician, auto dealer, attorney, radio announcer, retired stockbroker, dentist, banker, teacher, pediatrician, union administrator, and newspaper reporter, to name a few. Their work would be laborious and time-consuming, but sworn into office on April 6, 1971, by Governor Guy, the assembled 98 commenced their work. Frank A. Wenstrom, Williston, served as president; William R. Pearce, Bismarck, as first vice president; Stanley Saugstad, Minot, as second vice president; and Lois Vogel, Fargo, as secretary.[165]

Committees on Education, Resources and Public Lands, Executive Functions, Taxation and Finance, Judicial Functions and Political Subdivisions, Legislative Functions, and the Preamble, Bill of Rights, and Suffrage came into existence shortly after Governor Guy called the first session of the convention to order.

As the "people" commenced their labors, a number of significant events took place, all causing the state and its residents to pause in their activities and wonder what the future held. Perhaps most disturbing changes occurred on the academic front. On January 9, 1970, fire destroyed the two main instructional and office buildings—Carnegie Hall and the Home Economics Building—at the University of North Dakota's Ellendale branch. Lost to the flames, the structures housed the biology, chemistry and physics laboratories, music practice areas, five general classrooms, a 300-seat auditorium, five administrative offices, ten faculty offices, and the bookstore.[166]

Established by the state's initial constitution in 1889, but not financed or constructed until 1899, the Ellendale Industrial School never quite lived up to the founding fathers' expectations. For several years, the campus provided the community as its final two years of high school. Even after being charged as a normal school, the campus never excelled, perhaps due in part to its rather isolated location, but also perhaps due to its relative closeness to such institutions of higher learning as North Dakota State University, Jamestown College, Valley City Normal School (State University), and South Dakota's Northern State Teacher's College.

Its burning, then, left the citizenry of North Dakota with a significant question. To close the institution would be in some sense to admit to their parents and grandparents that they had once been far too optimistic with regard to the state's future population and needs or as Elwyn Robinson would refer to the case: "The Too Much Mistake."[167]

While some called for a reprieve, as well as a rededication to the spirit of founders, and evoked images of phoenixes rising from the ashes, others took a more clear-eyed view of the situation. The enrollment at the Ellendale campus never exceeded 200 students and then only after the industrial school became a normal school and fell under the guidance of the University of North Dakota. Accreditation of programs became problematic with declining numbers, as well as the will of the state to support the institution. Discussion of turning the institution into a community college with a two-year educational mandate played loudly in the ears of taxpayers. Every solution seemed to be far too costly for the benefit received. For some, then, the fire of January 1970 seemed providential.[168]

In the primary election of September 1972, voters moved to remove mention of the Ellendale campus from the state constitution, in essence disestablishing the institution. The retrenching vote could not be considered close; 68,575 individuals voted to close the school and 41,350 voted to maintain it. Later that year, the state sold remaining campus to Trinity Bible College, associated with the Assemblies of God Church, for $1 and the promise to maintain the structures, if not upgrade them.[169]

As society underwent its wrenching changes in the early 1970s, a continuation of the latter 1960s, the University of North Dakota did not fall exempt. After the May 4, 1970, shootings at Kent State University in Ohio, where National Guardsmen shot and killed four students, Grand Forks campus leaders called for a day of mourning to be held May 5, 1970. Administration officials cancelled classes for the event, perhaps sensing the tension that pervaded the campus. Outside of Twamley Hall, the primary administration building on the UND campus, a crowd estimated between 1,500 and 2,000 gathered. Speeches and a rock band dominated the proceedings, although some students attempted to speak out against the government, the war in Vietnam, and the general state of the nation. Most of the attendees appeared more interested in events than active in them. When a small group of individuals turned their attention to the campus armory, a window in a door broke, possibly by a thrown rock, possibly by accident. The students who were present immediately took up a collection to pay for the damage.[170]

The following day, while some encouraged the closure of the campus, the majority of students returned to their classes, preparing for the end of the semester examinations and the freedom of the forthcoming summer. Elsewhere on campus, for the first time, the administration recognized an organization of African American students, as well as one of Native American students. Feminist concerns brought the Women's Center.[171]

Still the Vietnam War gripped the consciousness of North Dakota's youth. Shortly after the Grand Forks incident, students from the University of North Dakota, determined to offer their opinion to the federal government by protesting the antiballistic facility then under construction near Nekoma. According to rumor, students from around the region, perhaps from as far away as the University of Minnesota, planned to gather at the University of North Dakota to trek as a unit to the remote site. With the possible demonstration only days away, Governor Guy wired President Richard Nixon of the potential protest, warning that the resources of the state could not be stretched so thin as to adequately protect the missile site and requesting federal assistance to do so. Guy informed the president that North Dakota authorities could only guarantee the safety of its citizens, not that of federal property.[172]

In response, United States Assistant Attorney General Richard Kleindienst dispatched a crew of Department of Justice officials to North Dakota, in part to persuade Guy to deploy the state's National Guardsmen, and in part simply to observe the happenings and report their findings to the president. Part of the happenings involved the level of radicalism present in North Dakota, and in order to address what appeared to be a growing element of discontent, Guy flew to Grand Forks to address several hundred students and faculty members. Promising that any National Guardsmen at the scene would not be carrying loaded weapons, Guy declared that potentially a limited number of guardsmen along the route from Grand Forks to Nekoma would be carrying loaded weapons in order to *protect* the protesters from molestation.[173]

United States Attorney General John Mitchell, furious with Guy for not bringing out the National Guard, then jumped into the fray. Guy adamantly refused to send North Dakota's National Guardsmen to protect the antiballistic missile site, proclaiming that the Guard's first responsibility lay with the protection of the state's citizenry and property, not the protection of the federal government's property. He averred that if the federal government so desperately sought protection for the Nekoma site, forces from the Grand Forks Air Force Base might be utilized as a police unit.[174]

Mitchell raged without success, giving up on his cause only when Guy informed him that he himself might be at the protest, not as an observer, but rather as "one more warm body" to stand beside those who saw the antiballistic missile site as a colossal waste of federal tax dollars. Besides, he strongly believed in the people's right to peacefully assemble and voice their concerns. Moreover, it appeared to Guy that the attorney general and the president wished to distance themselves from any potential violence by using state troops rather than federal ones should they be needed to quell any disturbances.[175]

While it was expected that individuals from North Dakota State University would join their colleagues from the University of North Dakota, as would students from Moorhead State College, where others might come from and their numbers remained somewhat of a mystery to all involved. Estimates ran wild. Would 8,000 attend Friday night's peace rally at Grand Forks? Would 5,000 or perhaps even 50,000 march on the Nekoma antiballistic site? State officials also had to wonder at the number of students who would attend an unassociated rock concert scheduled for that same Saturday at Turtle River State Park. Would the two events meld, creating a synergy of uncontrollable proportions? Officials need not have worried as much as they did.[176]

May 16 proved to be a sodden day, making the trek to the actual site a difficult one. Vehicle after vehicle became stuck in the mud as the day progressed. Ever thoughtful,

Guy had arranged for two tow trucks to be present to provide free assistance for those who became stuck. No farmer would be called upon to provide service to those who might be damaging his fields and driveways by their actions. And, just in case, the National Guard was mobilized for weekend duty, albeit not at the Nekoma site, but rather scattered at various locations throughout the northeastern portion of the state. While the presence of National Guardsmen had been kept somewhat quiet in relation to the Zip to Zap of the previous year, Guy made no effort to hide the fact that troops would be in the vicinity.[177]

The rain kept numbers down. An estimated 1,000 to 1,500 students made the trip from Grand Forks to Nekoma, peace prevailing. Following a song fest, a tree planting, and a few speeches, the crowd dispersed. The area was clear by no later than 4 P.M. The Turtle River State Park concert, however, attracted a few more rowdy individuals, perhaps as many as 5,000 in total, requiring a few arrests for vandalism and drunkenness. The weekend had cost the state of North Dakota approximately $58,000, but peace triumphed and the federal government's overwhelming concerns had not been borne out by the residents of North Dakota and the surrounding regions.[178]

In comparison with the staunch isolationist movements of the past, *most* North Dakotans seemingly paid limited attention to the war in Vietnam. Sentiment against World Wars I and II, as well as the Korean War, clearly held against involvement. But then, the isolationist voices of William Langer, William Lemke, Gerald Nye, and the Scandinavian immigrants of old had been silenced by time. During the course of the war, approximately 200 young men gave their lives for their country.[179]

Although men and women from North Dakota served in the Vietnam War, others spent the Vietnam War in North Dakota, staffing Minot and Grand Forks Air Force Bases. At Minot, in an effort at modernization, the United States Air Force selected the 91st Strategic Missile Wing to become the first to convert to the Minuteman III intercontinental ballistic missile. This particular missile tripled the striking power, significantly elevating the credibility of the Strategic Air Command as a deterrent to possible attack by the Soviet Union. Grand Forks Air Force Base also upgraded its missile allotment to the Minuteman III during the 1970s.[180]

If money flowed into the state for the armed forces and defensive structures, it did not do likewise for the massive water projects associated with Garrison Dam and its diversion. Although modestly funded in 1969, the McClusky Canal, meant to move water from the Missouri River to the central portion of the state and to stretch some 74 miles from Lake Audubon to the headwaters of the Sheyenne River, never proved its worth by carrying water to the east. Voice after voice rose against the project: the Committee to Save North Dakota, the North Dakota Farmers' Union, the North Dakota Fish and Wildlife Service, the Audubon Society, and the Canadian government, all railed against the project as expensive, environmentally unsound, and simply unnecessary. With federal dollars not flowing to the canal, work came to a halt in 1976.[181]

Other environmental concerns rose to the fore with the mining of lignite coal. Lignite coal burns with less sulfur emissions than other kinds of coal. Accordingly, the 350,000,000,000 tons of it beneath the surface of North Dakota became an issue in the energy-strapped 1970s. To some, the idea of unrestricted mining, forever altering the landscape of the state, could not be brooked. How should it be controlled? What should happen to the surface of the land in the aftermath of strip mining? Should the state extract a higher tax on the coal, which would one day, of course, no longer be available? What of the energy that North Dakotans themselves required?[182]

Clearly a multiplicity of issues faced the electorate as the elections of 1972 came into view. The first of these to be addressed had to be the Constitutional Convention. Shortly after Governor Guy called the first session of the convention to order on April 6, 1971, Committees on Education, Resources and Public Lands, Executive Functions, Taxation and Finance, Judicial Functions and Political Subdivisions, Legislative Functions, and the Preamble, Bill of Rights, and Suffrage came into existence. These groups toiled independently over the course of the next year, often meeting for two- or three- day sessions. The assorted committees collected testimony, gathered memoranda, and studied the background of various issues in hopes of making informed decisions. Moreover, the committees met with citizen groups scattered in 16 locations throughout the state. Citizens suggested at least one hundred ideas that they believed should be incorporated into the new constitution.[183]

On January 3, 1972, the convention met in plenary session to labor for 30 days of discussion on what each of the committees had produced. On February 17, the convention voted on their handiwork. With three members absent, and four voting against the draft, it passed with a total of 91 supporting conventioneers. The public awaited its opportunity to speak. Before the special election called for the purpose of ratifying the new constitution, delegates covered the state, explaining the document, urging its passage.[184]

While North Dakotans supported the calling of the constitutional convention, not all liked what it had produced. Members of the AFL-CIO as well as the National Farmers' Organization, in particular found the document wanting. Both organizations lobbied against adoption on the grounds that the constitution maintained North Dakota as a "right-to-work" state, limiting the power of organized labor. Rural Electric Associations (REAs) lobbied against the constitution as well. They felt, or as Guy came to believe, that the new constitution held against the cooperative movement. The debate against the constitution, limited for the most part to the two weeks prior to the special election, proved successful. On April 28, 1972, the proposed constitution met with sound defeat. On a vote of 107,643 to 64,073, constituents determined to stay with the constitution that had governed them since the inception of statehood.[185]

With the failure of the constitution, ancillary measures on the ballot mattered little, except to illustrate the mind of the voters. Along with the constitution's defeat, North Dakotans voted against giving full adult status to 18 to 20-year-olds, against a unicameral form of legislative assembly, for allowing the legislature to determine whether or not lotteries and gift enterprises should be allowed, and favored an increase in the signature requirements for initiated and referred matters.[186] For Guy, a strong supporter of the proposed constitution, "it was a real sad day."[187]

Soon upon the heels of the voters' determination upon the constitution came the general election of 1972. Governor William Guy, having served twelve years and having been elected for two 2-year and two 4-year terms, made the decision not to run again for the state's highest office. Arthur A. Link stood for election for the Democratic-NPL Party. Previously serving in the United States House of Representatives from the western district of the state, he realized that with the consolidation of the state into a single congressional district, his job could not be considered secure. Convinced by colleagues to run for the governorship, Link defeated former Lt. Governor Republican Richard F. Larsen.[188]

Link, the son of immigrant homesteaders from Bohemia, became known during his terms of office, as a fiscal conservative who advocated the responsible, careful use of the state's natural resources at a time when the worldwide energy crisis encouraged the opposite. Staunchly pro-life, deeply religious, devoted to the youth of the state (despite their calls for a lowered drinking age), Link oversaw the state during some of its most troubled financial times, particularly as related to the faltering agricultural economy. Despite calls upon the state to raise taxes, Link avoided doing so by enforcing stringent measures of economy, but still managing to build upon the state's quality educational structure.[189]

The state's single member of the United States House of Representatives became Republican Mark Andrews, a Cassleton farmer. Andrews had served in the House since a special election elevated him to the position in 1963 upon the death in office of Hjalmer C. Nygaard. And, although not standing for election, North Dakota's senators remained Milton C. Young and Quentin N. Burdick, Republican and Democrat, respectively.[190]

U.S. Representative Mark Andrews

U.S. Senate Historical Office

Senator Milton R. Young

U.S. Senate Historical Office

On the presidential front, North Dakotans voted overwhelmingly for Republican Richard M. Nixon, supporting his reelection campaign with 174,109 votes compared to the 100,384 that they gave to Democratic candidate South Dakotan George McGovern.[191] In consideration of state, local, and national politics, by all definitions, the state remained a two-party one during the 1960s and early 1970s.

On the same day that North Dakotans elected the second consecutive Democrat to the governor's mansion, they voted on an initiated measure: whether or not to allow physicians to perform abortions under certain preconditions. Overwhelming, the populace voted against the measure: 62,604 in favor to 204,852 against.[192]

One of North Dakota's stranger moments came during 1973. At the onset of the school year, parents and school board officials at Drake became upset with one teacher's assignment of Kurt Vonnegut's *Slaughterhouse-Five,* citing the volume's "unwholesomeness," perhaps referring to the single line "Get out of the road, you dumb motherfucker," as spoken to an unarmed American chaplain's assistant during the Battle of the Bulge. Regardless of the line that upset so many, the response was not one that made all North Dakotans proud. Not only was the English teacher who assigned the volume fired from his position, but the school custodian burned 32 copies of the offending text in the school incinerator.[193]

As books burned, the race for to represent North Dakota in the United States Senate heated up. Governor William Guy had foregone the opportunity to serve a fifth term as governor, something he surely would have won had he contested for it, to make a run for the Senate. Standing between him and an address in Washington, D.C., stood long-term Senator Milton R. Young. Having been appointed to the Senate in 1945 to complete the term of the recently deceased John Moses, the Republican had remained in office, consistently reelected every six years. In 1974, despite being 76 years old, Young announced his intent to run for yet another term.[194]

The campaign settled into a vigorous fuss over age: Young proclaiming that Guy, at 55, did not have sufficient time remaining in his career to build up significant seniority for the benefit of the state, and Guy gently arguing that not only did the seniority system of the United States Senate not make sense, but that despite his renown physical fitness, perhaps Young had sufficiently served his state.

Unchallenged in the primary, Young saved his cash and energy for the general election. Guy challenged at the primary level by Robert McCarney, hemorrhaged cash in attempts to rebut full-page advertisements attacking his record as governor, his stance on the issues of the day, and his family. One advertisement slyly suggested that Guy had procured prostitutes for Vice President Hubert Humphrey and his entourage during a 1968 tour of the state. While ultimately triumphing over McCarney, Guy's uphill battle commenced early.[195]

Having secured the Democratic nomination, Guy soon realized he did not face only Young as a competitor. James Jungroth, formerly state Democratic chairman, determined to run for the office as an independent. Focusing his campaign almost entirely upon Guy's supposed record as an anti-environmentalist, Jungroth labored on the state's college campuses to paint himself as the protector of North Dakota's natural beauty and resources.

On the day following the election, the identity of North Dakota's second senator—the first being Quentin Burdick—had not been determined. The race hinged on less than a few hundred ballots, which automatically triggered a recount. In early December, Young again claimed his seat, but by a mere 186 votes of 235,661 cast. Jungroth's 6,739 votes gained as an independent swung the election.[196] Jungroth's nearly 7,000 votes did more than swing the election, however; they also illustrated the strong entrenchment of the two-party structure in North Dakota. Moreover, that his primary campaign issue focused on the environment could only be considered as radical, at least by North Dakota standards. It did, however, portend serious forthcoming questions about the natural environment as an energy crisis loomed and the farm front began to show troubling trends.

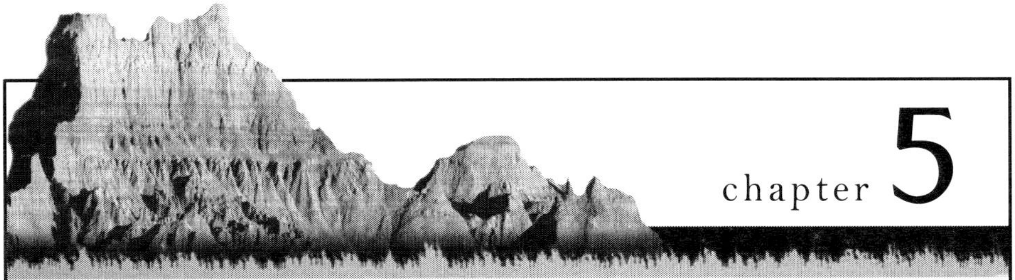

chapter 5

THE WORST OF TIMES AND THE BEST

The Latter 1970s

When Senator Milton R. Young prepared to take the oath of office in early 1975, commencing his sixth and final term in the United States Senate, North Dakotans had reason to celebrate. Not only had their long-term senator maintained his vaunted seniority on significant Senate committees, in addition, the state's economy, buoyed by rising agricultural prices and concomitant rural wealth, appeared sound. Record prices came as regularly as the harvest for the first years of the decade. Even the much discussed and bemoaned movement by the Organization of Petroleum Exporting Countries (OPEC) to cut oil sales to nations that supported Israel and its increase in prices of some 400 percent did not seem to harm the economy substantially.[197] Indeed, in the immediate aftermath of the OPEC announcement, oil production in North Dakota actually declined, albeit marginally, from 20.6 million barrels in 1972 to 20.2 million barrels in 1973, to 19.7 million barrels in 1974, only to rise slightly in the aftermath: 20.5 million barrels in 1975, 21.7 million barrels in 1976, and 23.3 million barrels in 1976.[198]

If oil production did not rise precipitously, lignite coal production did during the latter 1970s. In 1970, slightly over 5 million tons of coal was brought to the surface and by 1975 a total of 7.1 million tons was mined. However, by 1978 nearly 13 million tons of lignite were brought to the surface. Approximately 85 percent of the lignite mined in North Dakota remained in North Dakota with 75 percent of it used for the generation of electrical energy.[199]

Not only had those directly involved in lignite mining, however, reaped the financial harvest. Implemented in 1975 and effective in 1976, the state instituted a coal severance tax. Initially set at 85 cents per ton, the tax brought considerable funding to the state for its one-time harvest. In fiscal year 1976, the severance tax brought $4.3 million to the state's coffers, in fiscal year 1977 $6.1 million, and in fiscal year 1978 $7.8 million. Also instituted by the 1975 legislature was the coal conversion facilities tax. Facilities that used coal to generate electrical energy in excess of 120,000 kilowatts were subject to a tax of .5 mills per kilowatt produced for sale.[200] Coal significantly contributed to the economic well-being of the state in the latter 1970s.

North Dakotans had reasons beyond a relatively sound economy to celebrate in the early days of 1975. Statistics gathered by assorted state and federal agencies showed a marked incline in the number of individuals calling North Dakota home. The census of 1970 had shown an alarming decrease of nearly 15,000 individuals from the preceding decennial census, most probably reflecting poor agricultural prices, low crude oil prices, and an abundance of opportunities elsewhere.

Now, however, things seemed to be turning around. Government statistics suggested that almost from the moment the 1970 decennial census was published, with the 1971 population estimated at 626,000 individuals compared to 1970's official count of 617,761 residents, a recovery of sorts had begun. By 1972, the population had risen to 632,000, by 1974 to an estimated 635,700, and by the start of 1975 to 636,900 individuals. An inclining population not only illustrated that fewer and fewer individuals left the farms and ranches of the state, but also that others had returned to the state in pursuit of profitable urban-oriented lives, either in manufacturing or service industries, while the United States Air Force also ensured that several thousand men and women called the state home, even if temporarily.[201]

Approximately 53 percent of North Dakotans, or about 337,500 individuals, classified themselves as rural in 1975. While not all of these residents could be called farmers, and indeed most were not, many made their living directly, or indirectly, from agricultural pursuits. Grain elevators, stockyards, implement dealers, hardware stores, banks, cafés, churches, newspapers, and schools could not function without the power of farmers and ranchers and their needs, as well as their disposable income. The actual number of farmers in North Dakota in the 1970s is somewhat difficult to pin down. In 1975 there were 43,000 farms/ranches throughout the state. However, claiming that there were therefore 43,000 farmers does not necessarily follow. On large, multigenerational operations, it is entirely feasible that more than one farmer/rancher contributed to the success of the enterprise. Nor does the number of farms/ranches take into consideration that both men and women can be farmers/ranchers, hence, essentially doubling the number of farmers/ranchers per operation, assuming a relatively high percentage of married agriculturalists.[202]

And agricultural incomes remained relatively high during the latter half of the 1970s, despite the pressures of increasing oil prices, chemical prices, farm implements, and land. Although the 1970s price of undifferentiated wheat had topped out at $4.09/bushel in 1974, and tumbled into the mid-$2/bushel range in the latter portion of the 1970s, the decade ended with wheat selling for an average of $3.78/bushel.[203] Durum prices also rode somewhat of a roller coaster in the latter half of the 1970s. In 1974, durum sold for $5.96/bushel; this, however, dropped to $2.69/bushel during the 1977 harvest, rising again to $4.35/bushel for the 1979 crop.[204]

For those farmers who raised corn as a primary crop, the roller-coaster effect could also be seen. In 1974, corn sold for approximately $3.02/bushel, falling to a low of $2.02/bushel for the 1977 crop, but rebounding to $2.52/bushel for the 1979 crop.[205] Soybeans, although somewhat limited in their North Dakota popularity as a cash crop, illustrated far less of the price variability of corn and wheat. For example, in 1974, soybeans sold for $6.64/bushel, falling to their lowest point of the latter half of the 1970s in 1975, returning only $4.92/bushel. By 1979, however, the price had rebounded to $6.28/bushel.[206]

Sunflowers, a relatively new cash crop for North Dakota, rose in popularity dramatically over the course of the 1970s. Used for both their oil and their edible qualities, sunflower prices only gained the United States Department of Agriculture's attention in 1975 for terms of historical reportage. Hence, the first available year of records is 1975 when North Dakota farmers averaged $10.80/cwt. Although the price rose to $11.00/cwt. the following year, by 1979, the price per hundred weight fell to $9.05. In 1978, sunflowers became the state's second largest cash crop, following only wheat in their significance to the agricultural economy.[207] Sugar beets continued their importance to the Red River Valley farmer, as did potatoes.

For ranchers, the trend for fat steer prices varied, but tended to move upward throughout the latter half of the 1970s. In 1974, fat steers had sold for $41.85/cwt. in the major United States markets. By 1976, this had fallen to $39.11/cwt. However, by the last year of the decade, fat cattle sold on major markets at a stunning $67.67/cwt., literally the highest prices ever recorded, albeit not adjusted for inflation.[208]

Despite relatively good prices for agricultural production, at least in comparison to years gone by, the farms and ranches of North Dakota did not hold all of their young men and women, nor for that matter all of their older men and women. Throughout the course of the 1970s, a variety of forces upon agriculture began a "shakeout" as the pressures of high inputs made some operations less than optimally profitable. Diesel and gasoline prices rose, as did the expenses of herbicides and insecticides, agricultural equipment, and the rate of interest charged on the operating loans assumed each spring in order to plant a crop. Farmers who had invested in land during the headier days of the early 1970s occasionally found themselves in financial difficulties, albeit not at the level that would occur in the 1980s.

Accordingly, the number of farms and ranches in North Dakota fell somewhat during the latter half of the 1970s, while the size of those operations remaining grew slightly. In 1974, approximately 43,000 farm operations tended the 41,700,000 acres of North Dakota's agricultural landscape, making for an average operation of 970 acres. Of course, *average* remains a dangerous word because it includes the Red River Valley farm of 640 acres, as well as the Slope County ranch of 10,000 acres. Regardless, in 1974 a whopping 92 percent of the surface area of the state was devoted to agricultural production.[209]

Over the course of the latter 1970s, the size of North Dakota's farms and ranches grew, while its number of agriculturalists fell. In 1975, the average farm/ranch in the state crossed the 1,000 acre barrier for the first time ever, while its number of operations fell to approximately 42,000 units, the lowest ever recorded in the twentieth century. By 1979, the number of farm and ranch operations fell to 40,500, but the size of the average operation rose to 1,030 acres. Clearly, despite reasonably good years on the agricultural front, changes were underway in the countryside.[210]

One of those changes came in the form of farmland prices. Throughout the early 1970s, prices trended upward. They continued to do so over the latter half of the 1970s as well. Southern Red River farmland that in 1975 sold for approximately $535/acre sold for $1,000/acre just four years later. In the northern valley, farmland that sold for $558/acre in 1975 met with $765/acre in 1979. Even the drier western lands, generally used only for grazing cattle, rose in value. In northwestern North Dakota, land that sold for $120/acre in 1975 sold for $245/acre in 1979. And in the southwestern quadrant, land that sold for $200/acre in 1975 fetched $265/acre in 1979. Coupled with issues related to crop price and increasing indebtedness for farmers as a whole, the most far-sighted individuals could see difficulties on the horizon.[211]

Over the course of the latter 1970s, the weather was not always kind to farmers or ranchers or for that matter North Dakota residents as a whole. In January 1975, a severe blizzard hit the state, as well as much of the upper Great Plains and upper Midwest. The storm rolled into North Dakota on Thursday, January 9, depositing 2 to 3 inches of fluffy snow, just perfect for blowing and drifting. On January 10, the true blizzard began: 35 to 45 mph wind gusts blew the previous day's snow, making visibility almost nonexistent. By Saturday, January 11, 65 mph wind gusts were not uncommon, and drifts piled high and then higher over the course of the weekend. Some drifts measured a full 12 feet deep.[212]

On Sunday, January 12, while some undoubtedly remained comfortably ensconced in their living rooms watching Super Bowl IX, in which the Pittsburgh Steelers beat the Minnesota Vikings 16–6 in balmy New Orleans, others turned to the massive cleanup of the cities, towns, and country roads of the northern portion of the state. Grand Forks officials predicted that it would take at least two weeks to clear the city's streets. No predictions appeared in the *Grand Forks Herald* as to the time it would take to clear the county's roads, to put Amtrak back in service, to start Greyhound routes again, or to ensure flights in and out of the local airport.[213]

While some dug out, or more sagely awaited snow plows and National Guardsmen to do the labor, others mourned their dead. At least a dozen North Dakotans lost their lives in the storm. Alfred Butler, a teenager, walked away from his car, stuck in the snow near Garske, and perished in the bitter winds. Similarly Peter Burghart, Jr., 34, from Wing, abandoned his car to walk for help and perished in the blizzard, as did Kathy Woyjick, 33, from Spiritwood. In Underwood, Barbara Saylor, 74, and her daughter Verna, 46, asphyxiated in their home due to difficulties with their furnace's ventilation system. Charles Miller, 84, in Minot suffered a similar fate. John Butz, 80, froze in his Felkirk home, while the body of James Ternes was found in his Bismarck apartment, its windows broken out, frozen. Ludwig Lornson, 92, in Coulee, also perished from exposure to the elements.[214]

Perhaps most disturbing, three young men simply disappeared enroute from Wahpeton to Crary to watch a basketball game on Friday, January 10. Despite air and ground searches, nothing of the men could be discovered, except their abandoned, snowbound automobile. Then, on the seventh day of the search, the bodies of Larry Michelson (Minot), Gary Adrian (Binford), and Larry Olson (Binford), were found frozen in a field some 2.5 miles from their car. The discovery of their bodies brought the state's death toll to an even dozen. The loss of livestock was incalculable.[215]

March 1975 brought another blizzard, albeit of rather minor proportions if compared to its predecessor. It left some 30 inches of snow, predominantly in the eastern portion of the state. The storm that lasted nearly five days left three North Dakotans dead in its wake.[216]

One significant result of the winter's blizzards came in the form of devastating floods along the Red River of the North. As the winter's accumulation of snow melted, the sodden ground could not begin to hold the moisture, nor could the Red River drain it northward with sufficient speed. Accordingly, the river rose, and then rose some more.

By April 23, the river ran through Grand Forks at 43.3 feet, flood stage being reached at 28 feet. Damages to urban areas, in 1975 dollars, reached $1.3 million. Rural damages ran much higher. North of Grand Forks, the river generally runs from 75 to 100 feet, bank to bank. In April 1975, however, it inundated areas, claiming a swath that occasionally topped 10 miles in width. Crop loss due to late planting, or no planting at all, as well as structural damage to farm homes and buildings and roadways totaled nearly $13 million.[217]

But the Red River was not done with North Dakota, or Minnesota, for 1975. In what can only be described as a freak occurrence, the Red rose from its banks a second time that year. During June 28 to 30, from 10 to 22 inches of rain fell on the southern end of the valley, landing on already saturated soils. With no place else to go, the precipitation made its way to the river. In Grand Forks, the crest came on July 14 at 43.08 feet. While urban damage was comparatively slight, rural damage was considerably worse than during the springtime flood. In consideration of crops lost on the over two million inundated acres, as well as to farmstead properties, machinery, and stored grains, the estimated damage to rural North Dakotans and Minnesotans rose to $238,800,000.[218]

If 1975 was wet and problematic, 1976 could only be declared dry and problematic. North Dakota averages, statewide, albeit with considerable variation from point to point, approximately 18 inches of precipitation annually. In 1975, nearly 21 inches of precipitation fell statewide, making it one of the more moist years in recent memory. However, in 1976 a mere 12 inches of precipitation fell statewide. It was the driest year since the legendary Dust Bowl years of the 1930s. With the exception of 1977, the wettest year on record, the remainder of the decade witnessed precipitation somewhat below the 50-year average.[219]

In a region so dependent upon the success of its farmers to bring success to its small towns, and ultimately to its larger communities, the weather can and does play a considerable factor in the state's economic well-being. That said, the Red River of the North was not yet done harassing the farmers, or the urban dwellers, of eastern North Dakota.

In 1978, following a winter of relatively substantial snowfall, the National Weather Service made the early prediction of flooding in the valley. While this gave urbanites some opportunity to prepare, their rural neighbors truly had no way to protect the majority of their assets from the forthcoming deluge. As the Red rose to its highest recorded levels of the century, farmers witnessed their homes and farm buildings, as well as their fields and roads suffer extensive damage. Over a half million acres flooded, resulting in nearly $13 million in damages to the economy.[220]

By the time the flood waters of 1979 receded, the flood of 1978 seemed like only the mildest of challenges. The winter of 1978–79 proved to be a difficult one: Temperatures remained below freezing for nearly five months; unusually heavy snowfalls repeatedly blanketed the area. However, when the thaw came in April 1979, it came with a vengeance. Not only did rains fall upon the already saturated landscape, but the melt came rapidly in a series of days reaching 50 to 60 degrees. Accordingly, the river rose rapidly, leaving little time for preventative measures against the floodwaters. By the time the waters receded, North Dakotans absorbed over $90 million in damages. Both rural and urban areas felt nature's wrath.[221]

The Vietnam War, wrath of an entirely different form, came to its conclusion in April 1975, leaving 198 North Dakota men dead or presumed so by their Missing in

Action (MIA) status.[222] While the numbers of North Dakota dead seemed small in comparison to the nation's loss of 58,000 dead, 300,000 wounded, 2,500 unaccounted for, 100,000 missing one or more limbs, and some 150,000 veterans suffering from drug or alcohol addiction or severe psychological disorders, the loss of a son, grandson, husband, nephew, paperboy, or pastor's son brought the distant war home to Lisbon, Langdon, Ft. Totten, Fessenden, Mandan, Mott, Rhame, Rugby, Napoleon, New England, Belcourt, and Belfield.[223]

Not specifically related to the conclusion of the Vietnam War, but still militarily oriented came the shocking news that the Stanley R. Micklesen Safeguard Complex that had been under construction near Nekoma, North Dakota, was to be deactivated. Built from funds appropriated in 1969 at the height of the Cold War, the complex brought the launch facilities for thirty Spartan and sixteen Sprint nuclear-tipped weapons. Four remote and unnamed sites hosted another fifty or so Sprint missiles. The facility's stated purpose was to serve as an antiballistic missile site, intercepting and destroying any nuclear weapons the Soviets might send our direction.[224]

Not only did the program bring missiles and a new lexicon to the eastern prairies of North Dakota, it also brought considerable funds for employees, materials, housing, roads, and so on. Of course, the funding for the missile site trickled into all areas of the economy as laborers spent their checks and suppliers expanded their workforce. President Richard Nixon had signed an appropriation bill for $137.8 million for the entirety of the project in 1969. Work commenced on the project in May 1970, backed by 2,626,200 pages of architectural drawings and 4,340,000 pages of specifications. Work came to its conclusion, and the site was considered operational on April 1, 1975.[225]

While of global importance, few North Dakotans could be blamed if they missed the local significance of President Nixon and Soviet General Secretary Leonid Brezhnev's signing of the May 26, 1972, Anti-Ballistic Missile Treaty. By the terms of the treaty, both the United States and the Soviet Union found themselves limited to a single site to protect strategic locales and another to protect the "National Command Authority." Despite the terms of the treaty, work continued on the 85 percent-completed Nekoma complex. Work on a similar site in Montana ceased.[226]

Nuclear tips for the majority of Spartan and Sprint missiles arrived in Nekoma in the early months of 1975, with the facility considered in operation on April 1 of that year. All 30 Spartan and 70 Sprint missiles were loaded for nuclear war by October 1975. Then came the strangest news of all. Just a single day after the Mickelsen complex became fully operational, the United States Congress voted to deactivate the system. The site had been in official operation a *single* day.[227]

Closure of the facility drastically changed the communities of Pembina and Cavalier counties. Writing in *The Nation*, Carey MacWilliams noted: "Safeguard played havoc with the lives and fortunes of the people of Langdon, ND....1,500 persons, about a third of Langdon's population, were employed in connection with the ABM. Many others had found work and business opportunities in the influx of capital surrounding the Safeguard's construction. Workers migrated from all over the country for jobs on the missile site. When Safeguard closes...Langdon will be hit by a depression made in Washington." Beyond those individuals who came to North Dakota to build the structure, others had planned on permanent employment at the site. An estimated 433 airmen and 108 civilians lost what had been presumed permanent jobs at the Mickelsen site.[228]

North Dakota, particularly the northeastern portion, felt the impact of the facility's closing almost immediately. By February 1976, unemployment in Pembina and Cavalier counties stood at 8.6 and 7.5 percent, respectively, far higher than the remainder of the state. A loss of $1.3 million in procurements affected Langdon, Walhalla, and Grand Forks. People flooded from the region, depleting the tax base. Population estimates ran from a 23 percent loss of population for Walhalla, for Osnabrock a 40 percent loss, for Cavalier and Elton a 43 percent loss, and for Mountain a 55 percent loss. Towns that had intended to profit by the site's presence for generations found themselves severely indebted for sewer and telephone systems. Individuals who had hoped to cash in on the Mickelsen site found themselves on the verge of bankruptcy for apartments built on speculation, restaurants opened in hopes of hungry laborers, and liquor licenses obtained for bars with the thought of thirsty workers. Schools in the Langdon area lost approximately 50 percent of their enrollment with the closure. The impact of the closure could scarcely be measured. The newspapers of North Dakota voted the facility's closing as the most significant news story of 1975.[229]

The political dynamics of North Dakota in the latter half of the 1970s continued to illustrate the growing strength of the two-party structure in the state. After years of inconsequential activity, a limited voice for the individuals who aligned themselves with the party, and electoral failure, the Democratic Party continued to show signs of strength on nearly every political level possible.

Governor Arthur Link, elected in 1972, continued in office, meeting the challenges of a state in transition. The worldwide energy crisis, although not dramatically or immediately impacting the state, did have larger ramifications. Predominantly, firms from across the United States turned to the state as a potential source of energy products: coal, natural gas, crude oil. A staunch conservationist, Link demanded that any efforts to claim the energy sources below the surface not permanently scar the landscape of the state. While some accused Link of standing in the way of progress, his efforts brought legislation requiring that firms extracting coal be required, as part of their contracts, to restore the surface of the land to its condition pre-extraction: land reclamation.[230]

Of his efforts, Link once wrote:

> *. . . And when we are through with that and the landscape is quiet again When the draglines, the blasting rigs, the power shovels and the huge gondolas cease to rip and roar! and when the last bulldozer has pushed the last spoil pile into place, and the last patch of barren earth has been seeded to grass or grain. Let those who follow and repopulate the land be able to say . . . Our grandparents did their job well. This land is as good and, in some cases better than before. Only if they can say this will we be worthy of the rich heritage of our land and its resources.*[231]

Coal and land reclamation did not absorb all of Link's time and energy. In the midst of his first term of office (1973–77), it became apparent that the nation needed more electrical power and natural gas, as well as coal and oil, than it had in previous years. Accordingly, a number of schemes came to the fore to slake those thirsts. While some solutions offered lay in coal being turned into electrical power, others lay in coal being turned into natural gas. Throughout the mid-1970s, various energy-oriented firms from across the nation hatched plans to capitalize on North Dakota's lignite. One of significance came from the Michigan-Wisconsin Pipeline Company, a subsidiary of American Natural Gas. The intent was to use lignite and large quantities of water to produce gasification plants in Beulah, Center, Washburn, and Dodge-Halliday, North Dakota. Optimists suggested that not only would dozens of electrical generation and gasification plants be constructed, but that the West River population would increase from about 86,000 to nearly a half million. Environmentalists found much to criticize in the plans. Not only would millions of gallons of water be diverted from their natural courses, but nearly 3 percent of the state's total surface would be mined in order to make everyone's plan a reality.[232]

Soon, however, another difficulty arose: financing. As firm after firm fell from contention for the appropriate permits to construct the coal gasification and electrical generation plants, ultimately only American Natural Gas and its subsidiary Michigan-Wisconsin Pipeline Company remained contenders. Then, in the latter 1970s, American Natural Gas, working with the state of North Dakota, offered up its plan. To construct a plant half the size of the original proposition would cost at least $600 million. Concerned that construction might never occur, North Dakotans, Link in particular, took the case for federal support to then-President Jimmy Carter. Ultimately, the Carter

Great Plains Synfuels Coal Gasification Plant, Beulah

Courtesy of Basin Electric Power Cooperative

administration provided a $240 million federal loan guarantee to commence construction, which began in early 1980.[233]

Other tasks before the governor included funding public kindergarten, finding additional support for the expansion of services to the developmentally disabled, encouraging the purchase of Cross Ranch (a large privately owned property south of Washburn where the Missouri River still ran untamed), and modernizing and expanding the State Mill and Elevator. He also created the North Dakota Bicentennial Committee to help the state celebrate the nation's 200th anniversary.[234]

Not all ran entirely smoothly for the governor, however. A devout Christian and staunch friend of the state's youth, he vetoed legislation that would have lowered the state's legal age for the consumption of alcohol from 19 to 18. His veto held and the youth of North Dakota did not particularly look kindly on him after that event. He noted in his retrospective on the governorship that he was asked to throw out the basketball at the Class A tournament. However, when he was given the ball at the start of the second half, he was soundly booed by the youth in attendance. For Link, the booing did not shake his faith in the veto. As he noted, after the basketball game and for a considerable time afterward, "many more people came around and [said] you did the right thing."[235]

Beyond the veto maintaining the age of legal alcohol consumption, other concerns gripped the state in the mid-1970s. Of particular interest was the federal Equal Rights Amendment. The proposed 27th Amendment to the United States Constitution needed the support of 38 state legislatures in order to become the law of the land. Reading simply: "Equality of rights under the law shall not be denied or abridged by the United States or by any state on account of sex. The Congress shall have the power to enforce by appropriate legislation, the provisions of this article," the proposed amendment created havoc throughout the land. Charges and countercharges, both true and false, followed in any discussion of the amendment.

North Dakota supporters of the amendment marshaled their forces early, determined to be one of the 38 states required to pass the Equal Rights Amendment. The Coordinating Council for the Equal Rights Amendment came into existence to see the bill through the legislature. Contributing forces to the Coordinating Council included the American Association of University Women, the League of Women Voters, the North Dakota Business and Professional Women's Clubs, Common Cause, and the North Dakota Education Association. Headquartered in Bismarck, the pro-ERA forces lobbied without pause for their cause. Ultimately, the North Dakota Senate passed the amendment 28 to 22, with the House passing the amendment by a one-vote margin. In an ultimately losing battle, North Dakota was the only state to ratify the Twenty-seventh Amendment in 1975.[236]

The role of women in North Dakota underwent substantial change over the course of the 1970s. While many older women remained homemakers and part-time assistants in family-operated ranches, farms, and businesses, more and more younger women were completing college and university degrees, making it possible for them to enter the ranks of the professions. Nursing, social work, and education no longer claimed all graduates, as they had for so many years. Women were entering the business world, owning and operating their own firms, or serving in the firms of others. Other women found the law or medicine to their liking, while others still entered politics.[237]

Throughout the 1920s, 1930s, 1940s, 1950s, and 1960s, exceptionally few women sought political office in North Dakota. Indeed, in the aforementioned decades, the number of women serving in the state legislature at any given time could be counted on the fingers of one hand, and often with fingers left over. However, with the start of the 1970s, more and more women ran for state legislature, and more and more won. In the election of 1972, twelve women won seats, while in the election of 1974, sixteen women did so. The trend continued with the election of 1976 when nineteen women took the oath of office, and in 1978 when twenty women did so. While still only a small percentage of the legislature, women clearly made an impact on state government in the 1970s.[238]

The election of 1976, a presidential election year, as well as a gubernatorial election year, provided few surprises. President Gerald Ford easily carried North Dakota over Georgia Governor Jimmy Carter, 153,470 to 136,078. Regardless of North Dakota's inclination to the Republican Party, the aftermath of Watergate and the pardon granted Richard Nixon upon his departure of the White House, did not sit well with many Americans, and nationwide, Carter defeated the Republican Ford, 40,825,839 to 39,147,770. On the gubernatorial level, Arthur A. Link, a Democrat, defeated Republican candidate Richard Elkin, 153,309 to 138,321.[239]

Link remembered that the Democratic convention and ensuing campaign flowed much more smoothly in 1976 than it had in 1972. Not only did he not face competition for the Democratic nomination, his nomination came by acclamation. For most North Dakotans, he was a known figure, his term had brought general prosperity to the state, and he had fulfilled the general contours of his 1972 promises.[240]

Quentin Burdick, a Democrat, retained his seat in the Senate, handily defeating Robert Stroup by a margin of over 70,000 votes. Mark Andrews also retained his seat in the House of Representatives, defeating Democrat Lloyd Omdahl by approximately 75,000 votes. Clearly North Dakota remained a two-party state, so much so that the North Dakota House of Representatives was split precisely in half between Democrats and Republicans.[241]

In a retrospective on his second term in office, Link suggested that the term ran more smoothly than his first. Projects commenced in his first four years came to fruition in his second. Final plans came together for the construction of the Heritage Center in Bismarck, as well as for the protection of the Cross Ranch, a privately held property abutting seven untamed miles of the Missouri River. He also appointed the first tribal chairpersons to the state's Indian Affairs Commission.[242]

The ever-active Robert P. McCarney absorbed some of the governor's time. Known for his flagrant use of the initiative and referendum, particularly as associated with taxation, McCarney proposed legislation to increase the taxes on corporations and to decrease them on individual taxpayers. The measure passed, leaving some individuals to suggest that the state's tax code owed more to McCarney than to the legislature.[243]

The Garrison Diversion Unit provided more than its share of headaches for the governor, the state's farmers and ranchers, and its nature lovers. Despite its approval in 1965, the project to move Missouri River water to the eastern portion of North Dakota had proven to be a hard task to complete. Not only did the price tag keep rising, but so did opposition to the plan. Throughout the early 1970s, a number of efforts were undertaken to stall, if not entirely discontinue, the project. The Committee to Save North Dakota had formed in 1972, requesting that further environmental impact studies be undertaken along the half-completed McClusky Canal. In 1973, the Canadian government made a formal request, asking for a moratorium on the continued construction of the diversion project until concerns could be addressed regarding microorganisms potentially flowing into Hudson Bay via the Red River of the North and the Souris River.[244]

Resistance to the Garrison Diversion continued well through the latter 1970s. Indeed, in 1976, the National Audubon Society sued the federal government, claiming that the environmental impact statement for the diversion contained numerous flaws. Problems continued for supporters of the diversion when in 1977 President Jimmy Carter slashed funding for the project to absolutely nothing. Only after significant protest did the president offer up continuation funds and only after recommending the irrigation field be shrunk from 250,000 acres to 96,000 acres. As well, the International Joint Commission on the project concluded that the risk of contaminating Hudson Bay by marine microorganisms was too high. It recommended that the waters that would eventually flow to Canada be eliminated from the project, in essence cutting the 250,000 acres to be irrigated by 87 percent, or down to only 32,500 acres.[245]

If the Garrison Diversion project left many in North Dakota frustrated, and even angry, the State Bank of North Dakota did not leave the state's residents with such frustration. Indeed, during the 1970s, the bank seemed to awaken from decades of quietude to decades of activity. The bank prospered during the 1970s, increasing profits by 201 percent over the decade. Its resources rose by an astounding 385 percent during the same time period. While maintaining its original purpose of providing low-interest loans to farmers, the bank also expanded its services to meet the needs of a late twentieth-century urbanizing state. It entered the marketplace to provide low-interest loans to individuals purchasing their homes via the Veterans' Administration or the Federal Home Association. It also started to underwrite student loans and, ultimately, to write student loans. It entered the arena of municipal bonds to aid communities in the construction of parks, drainage projects, sanitary sewer structures, roadways, and waterworks, among other projects. It also remained true to its roots, providing traditional agricultural loans, as well as loans specifically geared towards beginning farmers and ranchers. Despite legislative inquiries about the role of a state-operated bank in a free market economy, the Bank of North Dakota prevailed, continuing to provide resources to develop the state.[246]

Clearly the 1970s brought considerable change to the state of North Dakota: agricultural successes, increasing oil revenues, a growing population, altered relations with the federal government, changing social values, and much more. With few exceptions, the 1970s had been relatively profitable ones for the state; indeed, to many it appeared that North Dakota had turned a significant corner in its development. That feeling would not hold for long: The 1980s loomed.

chapter 6

IT ALL DEPENDS ON YOUR PERSPECTIVE

The Early 1980s

For the most part, the 1970s proved to be good years for the majority of North Dakotans: In general, agricultural prices rose, coal and oil extraction increased, the population swelled, the state's bank and elevator prospered (returning a fine profit to state coffers), and a two-party system fell firmly into place. The 1980s, however, offered few such comforts, particularly on the farm front.

At the time of the official decennial census of 1980, the state's population stood at 652,717, a handsome rebound of 5.7 percent from the 617,792 counted in 1970. The statistics illustrated that more and more individuals called urban locales home; 318,310 residents claimed to live in a community of 2,500 or more, up 16.4 percent from the previous census. The number living in communities of less than 2,500 stood at 334,407, a decline of 2.9 percent. Statewide, the number living in rural areas versus urban areas equalized. Forty-nine percent of North Dakotans claimed an urban residence and 51 percent claimed a rural one.[247]

Growth, however, did not come evenly across the state in terms of population. Indeed, the exodus from rural areas continued, as more and more North Dakotans sought the opportunities of an urban life: career, entertainment, cultural events, and so on. Burleigh County, home to the state capital, increased by 35 percent; Grand Forks County, home to the University of North Dakota and the Grand Forks Air Force Base, expanded by 8 percent; and Cass County, home to Fargo and North Dakota State University, rose by 20 percent. Mercer, Morton, McLean, and Oliver counties, all rich with coal and natural gas deposits, grew as well. However, many of the traditional farming counties of the central portion of the state lost population. Barnes County lost 7 percent of its population, Steele County 17 percent of its population, and Wells County 11 percent of its population.[248]

Of the state's population, 20,120 individuals claimed to be of Native American stock. Tribes were not recorded separately; hence, no detailed accounting of the Chippewa, Arikara, Hidatsa, Teton Lakota, or any other group can be separated out for detailed study. African Americans constituted a mere 2,568 residents, with Asian-based populations scarcely registering on the reports. Strangely, given its relatively small proportion of North Dakota's residents, individuals of Spanish heritage were singled out for special attention with regard to population, education, housing, occupation, nation of origin, fertility, and so on. Nearly 4,000 Spanish-origin individuals called North Dakota home at the time.[249]

For the first time in many years, the decennial census of 1980 recorded the occupation of the individuals enumerated. In 1980, 287,585 individuals over the age of 16 labored. The number of women working outside the home reflected a significant change in North Dakota's social structure. In 1970, only 72,961 women worked outside the home for pay. The number of women working for pay—113,868 doing so in 1980—rose by 56 percent over the decade, far exceeding the increase in population, and potentially marking several turning points in North Dakota's history.[250]

Not only were more and more women attending institutions of higher education, they found employment in seemingly nontraditional fields: medicine, law, government service, banking, and manufacturing, as well as in the more traditional fields of education, nursing, social work, and secretarial service. Moreover, women were marrying at a slightly older age and bearing fewer children. Feminist movements in the 1960s and 1970s provided women with permission if not the impetus to delay marriage, bear fewer children, and work for their own enjoyment. Additionally, more women found themselves *needing* to work in order not only to maintain a style of living, but rather to maintain a living at all. Stagflation, a slowed economy coupled with inflationary tendencies, reached North Dakota in the closing years of the 1970s.[251]

Men, of course, worked as well, but in a growing number of fields. Of the 173,717 men over the age of 16 employed in the state, many found employment in managerial positions, sales, service, construction, manufacturing, and transportation. The largest single occupational category, however, could not be considered a surprise. Of the men at work, 37,398 labored on farms and ranches, along with 3,654 of their female colleagues. Of course, the number of women working on ranches and farms beside their husband or father, but declaring themselves to be without occupation cannot be calculated.[252]

In the northern end of the Red River Valley, farmland that sold for $765/acre in 1979 sold for $909/acre in 1984. Generally, however, the trend in farmland prices was downward in the early 1980s. Southern Red River farmland that in 1979 sold for approximately $1,000/acre just five years later sold for $951/acre. Even the drier western lands, generally used only for grazing cattle fell in value. In northwestern North Dakota land that sold for $245/acre in 1979 sold for $132/acre in 1984. And in the southwestern quadrant, land that sold for $265/acre in 1979 fetched a mere $142/acre in 1984.[253]

As Jerome E. Johnson, author of the report, noted in his commentary, the decline in prices recorded in 1984 "reflected both a continued decline in demand for farmland and growing financial stress in the farm sector."[254] The mildly termed "growing financial stress in the farm sector" could clearly be seen in the number of farmers and ranchers in North Dakota, as well as in the average-sized operation. From 1979, when 40,500 operators controlled some 41,700,000 acres for an average farm size of 1,030 acres, the size of farms grew while the number of operators dropped. In 1982, 37,000 farmers and ranchers tended to 41,000,000 acres, resulting in an average farm size of slightly over 1,100 acres. By 1984, 35,500 individuals operated 41,000,000 acres, bringing the average farm size in North Dakota to 1,155 acres.[255]

As in the decades previous, wheat remained king of the commodities produced in North Dakota. Wheat, undifferentiated, sold for $3.91/bushel at the start of the 1980s, but fell in value nearly every year of the decade following. Durum did likewise, starting the decade at $5.00/bushel, falling to $3.75/bushel by the midpoint of the 1980s. It would fall even lower before the decade drew to its close, bottoming out in 1986 at a mere $2.70/bushel.[256]

Other crops vacillated in price over the course of the decade, but for the most part trended lower, particularly in the latter half of the decade. Corn, for example, started the decade at an average price of $3.11/bushel, falling to $2.63/bushel by 1984. Soybeans also fell throughout the decade, starting in 1980 at $7.57/bushel, but dropping to $5.05/bushel by 1985. Moreover, the price North Dakota farmers received for the sunflowers declined precipitously over the 1980s. In 1980, a hundred pounds of sunflower seeds sold for $11.10, on average. However, by 1985, farmers received only $7.93/cwt. Sugar beets started the decade at $47.20/ton, but at the midpoint of the decade brought their producers a mere $33.80/ton.[257]

Beef farmers also felt the pinch of the 1980s. While steers sold for $67.67/cwt. in 1979, they fell all the way to $62.52 in 1983, and by 1985 sold for only $58.34.[258] Of course, despite the declining market prices for agricultural products, the inputs required to produce a harvest did not decline. Fuel prices rose as the Oil Producing Exporting Countries (OPEC) tightened their grip on the world's oil production, as did the price of fertilizer, insecticides, herbicides, equipment, repairs, and taxes. Problems loomed, and loomed large. Many of the signs of distress could have been read in the closing days of the 1970s.

With a seemingly unquenchable foreign appetite for American grains, the Federal Land Bank, its lending restrictions recently removed, allowed farmers to incur substantial debt, as did other lending institutions. The result produced exponentially rising land prices as farmers sought to cash in on a perpetually rising market. Farm incomes rose above the national average in nine of the decade's years. The dreams of the 1970s, however, were not borne out by the realities of the 1980s.[259]

The realities of the 1980s started to become clear as early as January 4, 1980, when President Jimmy Carter announced a series of sanctions against the Soviet Union in retaliation for that nation's invasion of Afghanistan. While some bemoaned that the United States would not be participating in the 1980 Olympics, farmers took note of the strict embargo of grains to the Soviets. However, over the course of the 1980s the loss of the Soviet market would prove to be only the proverbial drop in the bucket to the economic conditions facing farmers. Throughout the 1970s, developing nations made large purchases of American grains. Yet over the early years of the 1980s the picture changed, and in a variety of ways. Nations that relied almost exclusively on the United States for their agricultural imports turned their attention to other sources, fearing that their own imports might someday be embargoed. Other developing nations indebted themselves so deeply to the United States that they were unable to meet repayment schedules and accordingly were forced to stop purchases from the nation all together. The rising value of the American dollar versus other currencies contributed to the surplus grain on the American market by making the nation's grain expensive, further lessening the demand for United States' commodities.[260]

Hence, by the early 1980s, the once-buoyant American agricultural economy started to sink. With lessening demand for grain, the price of farmland began to falter, slowly at first, and then in a freefall. Some federal officials estimated that land prices throughout the Midwest dropped by nearly 60 percent from 1981 to 1985. Prices for farmland did not reach their nadir until 1986.

As farmland prices declined, its value as collateral fell as well. Nationally, farmers owed an estimated $215 billion in early 1984, double the debt of 1978. Accordingly, lenders throughout the United States were called upon to reduce farmers' indebtedness in order that the value of their land might serve as sufficient collateral. Farmers across the United States struggled to repay their debt's interest, let alone the principal. Bankers and lenders, once popular as the source of cash that would make a farmer's dreams come true, became the symbol of personal failure, as they sought to recoup the losses their banks faced.[261]

Farmers did not face their troubles in isolation. The American Agriculture Movement, founded in the 1970s, briefly stirred to life to sponsor "tractorcades" on America's largest cities, including Washington, D.C., encouraging a grassroots response to the crisis. Similarly, the North American Farm Alliance coalesced in Ames, Iowa, to raise awareness of agricultural conditions among governmental officials and urban dwellers. Funds raised by country music star Willie Nelson in a series of Farm Aid concerts helped the United Farmer and Rancher Congress. Elsewhere farmers protested at bank-required foreclosure sales, occasionally with violence.[262]

Not only farmers felt the effect of their economic woes. As farmers had less and less disposable income, agribusiness felt an immediate impact: Implement dealers, seed houses, and elevators closed their doors in the face of the farmers' financial difficulties. Following shortly thereafter, grocery stores, furniture stores, banks, and hardware stores, among others, closed up shop, forced out by the economic decline of their regions.

Even harder hit were the churches, schools, homemaker clubs, and other assorted population-based organizations that dotted the countryside. As more and more farmers left the land for urban occupations, their children no longer attended rural schools, their families no longer attended rural churches, their wives found jobs in town leading to the disbanding of women's clubs, and the baseball diamonds, football fields, and 4-H clubs dwindled and then fell silent, no longer needed in regions facing serious out migration.

The federal government did not sit idle during the 1980s and watch while the nation's farmers struggled through another of their perennial crises. Some legislative endeavors that meant to aid the nation's agriculturalists became law; however, some Department of Agriculture actions resulted in deepening the disaster. For example, in 1980, the Department of Agriculture, facing its own budget constraints, determined to cut so-called entitlement programs: school lunch and breakfast programs, pre-natal nutrition programs such as Women, Infants and Children (WIC), food stamps, and Commodity Food Distribution. Not only were recipients hurt, so were the farmers who produced the "excess" products given away, further lessening their markets.[263]

The tight money policy practiced by the Reagan administration did not particularly aid farmers. With 60 percent of the nation's food and fiber production consumed within the United States, the farmers' welfare depended in large part upon the purchasing power of the American consumer. Tight money meant less disposable income for all, but as urbanites trimmed back their meat, breadstuffs, and vegetable consumption, farmers felt the sting. Other farmers felt the sting of being deemed too small for federal assistance. By the early 1980s, 17 percent of farmers received 60 percent of all agricultural subsidies paid by the federal government. Those farms generally were large-scale operations, and the plan generally left small-to-medium scale operators without the resources to continue in agriculture. More and more left the farm for urban occupations.[264]

Much of the farmland sold in the 1980s to satisfy mortgages did not fall into the hands of small-to-medium scale farmers. Rather, the land fell to foreign investors, nonagriculturalists, or large-scale farmers. With the Farm Credit System's rules that the land it had foreclosed upon could be purchased at 4.9 percent interest with 40 percent of the purchase price paid immediately, they were the only ones capable of meeting the demands. Accordingly, insurance companies more than doubled their land holdings from 1985 to 1986, and investor-owned farm management companies increased their holdings by 36 percent between 1979 and 1987.[265]

In order to face the exigencies forced upon them, many farmers turned to alternative crops. Artichokes, catfish, wildflowers, herbs, crayfish, honey, and garden truck were all touted as the solution to the farmers' woes, as were llamas and alpacas. Still, most farmers maintained their traditional crops: ones the federal government would subsidize, and once that added to the surplus of grains already on the market.[266]

Also adding to the surplus was the introduction of biogenetic seed stock. Grain stock was modified to be more resistant to disease, as well as to tolerate chemicals, that is herbicides, fungicides, and insecticides, used during the growing season. Superior yields resulted, often making government programs to reduce grain surpluses impotent. Genetically modified livestock became available to farmers, allowing them to market their livestock sooner, on less feed and inoculated to encourage growth.[267]

The federal government sought other avenues of surplus reduction throughout the 1980s, including Secretary of Agriculture John Block's Payment in Kind (PIK) endeavor. PIK, referred to by President Reagan as a "crop swap" whereby farmers would take land out of production and then receive not only cash payment, but also a payment in grain, which they could then sell on the open market. As a tool to aid farmers, the program was accepted as an emergency program. The general public was not so acquiescent. As land was taken out of production, tenant farmers and farm laborers lost their livelihoods, implement and fertilizer dealers were bereft of customers, and taxpayers were left with ever-increasing taxes in order to support grain prices, even with PIK in place.[268]

Despite the failure to elevate farm prices, the image of the farmer rose during the 1980s. As the decade wore on, more and more nonfarmers came to support higher taxes as way to preserve a viable agricultural economy. Slightly over 50 percent declared they would pay more in taxes to help farmers keep their land. Clearly, a corner had been turned with regard to the image of the farmer and farming. While negative images of farmers had prevailed throughout much of the twentieth century, the image now shifted to a more positive view. Hugh Sidey, once an Iowa farm boy himself, noted that farmers now seemed to enjoy a "deep reservoir of good will among the general public":

We are talking about people who want to give birth and grow and love and laugh and die, bonded and sustained by the soil, which is the oldest way of life Americans know. The farm economic crisis has become a rural crisis, and that has become a cultural crisis unique in our history. It is now beyond bank loans and government subsidies. It is in people's hearts.

Prosperous neighbors feel guilty. Bankrupt neighbors feel ashamed. Farmers who can afford new machines won't buy them, lest they embarrass friends. Machinery dealers go broke. Bankers anguish and hesitate—and fail.

The critical time is here. Can something that is old and beautiful and basic be saved by melding it with a lot that is new and brassy and unproven? The sociologists, historians and anthropologists are lined up, looking over the shoulders of the politicians, because something terribly important in American history is happening, and nobody knows how it is going to come out.[269]

The individual who most rapidly came to mind when North Dakotans stopped to contemplate the farm crisis, and sought someone to blame, was Democratic President Jimmy Carter. Guilty by association, Democratic Governor Arthur A. Link felt some of the animosity as well. Link, in a show of party solidarity, not only supported Carter's reelection bid, but also appeared publicly with the president as both campaigned for a return to office. For many, the Democrats' twenty-year hold on the governorship of North Dakota was enough. Allen I. Olson, Republican attorney general for the entirety of Link's time as governor, even coined the phrase "Twenty is Plenty" as he campaigned for the governorship himself.[270]

Governor Allen I. Olson

State Historical Society of North Dakota, D0723

Beyond the concept of one political party maintaining two decades of hegemony, Olson campaigned on the issue that Link's devotion to the severance tax for coal mining could only be construed as a stance against economic development. Link, however, contended that coal, a one-time harvest mined and often exported to Minnesota in the form of electricity, required a stiff severance tax, since it could never yield its wealth to the state again. Moreover, to harvest the coal without serious efforts at land reclamation shortchanged the future of North Dakota's youth in the form of a ravaged landscape.[271]

His ties to President Carter, the continuous holding of the governorship by Democrats for twenty years, a tradition of turnover in the office, the exceptional popularity of Republican Ronald Reagan and the ultimate pessimism that gripped the nation during the economic slowdown brought on by OPEC, the onset of the farm crisis, and the Iran hostage crisis combined for a perfect storm to sink Link's political hopes.

Allen I. Olson, a youthful 42 at the time of the campaign, won the governorship by a margin of approximately 22,000 votes—162,230 to 140,391 over Link. Olson's cabinet was entirely Republican in makeup, and the state swept another Republican, Mark Andrews, to the United States Senate in a landslide against Democratic challenger Kent Johanneson, 210,347 to 86,658. The Senate opening came as a result of Milton R. Young's determination to retire following his fifth term of office. Andrews's role as the state's only legislator in the United States House of Representatives undoubtedly aided his cause. Andrews's slot in the House of Representatives was filled by Democrat Byron Dorgan, most recently the State Tax Commissioner.[272]

On the national level, Republican Ronald Reagan swept Democratic incumbent Jimmy Carter from office on a vote of 43,899,248 to 35,481,435, with Independent John Anderson gaining 5,719,437 votes. In North Dakota, Reagan's margin of victory was resounding, 193,695 to 79,189, with Anderson gaining 3,743 votes.[273] As with Link, Carter's embargo of wheat to the Soviet Union cost him dearly in the eyes of the Flickertail State's electorate. The state's tradition of trending Republican in presidential elections also aided in the coming of the Reagan Revolution.

Of North Dakota's most recent governors, it does not take a great deal of imagination to declare Olson's term of office problematic. The farm crisis continued its grip upon the state, forcing farmer upon farmer from the land, and ultimately affecting every village and town in the state. Moreover, for the majority of his term in office, drought, albeit mild to that which would hit North Dakota in the closing years of the decade, dulled the landscape.[274]

Perhaps the most controversial feature of Olson's term of office came with a lawsuit filed against the state by the Association of Retarded Citizens (ARC). Overcrowding and untrained staff, as well as outdated attitudes towards the mentally challenged, combined to make the Grafton State School and the San Haven Institute a chamber of horrors. Patients routinely suffered abuse at the hands of those hired to care for their needs. In 1977, an unattended woman was scalded to death in a bathtub, while just two years later six employees were terminated for slapping hitting, kicking, and teasing residents for several months. When patients soiled themselves, the attendants often used a stiff brush to scrub their rectal areas. Patients suffered broken bones, bruises, and neglect; some committed suicide. One woman suffered rape at the hands of a diagnosed sexual predator.[275]

In order to control overpopulated wards, patients often received tranquilizers they did not need. Other residents of the facility found themselves restrained by blue-and-white fabric straps, which after being tied around their waists, looped through notches in a white board, then bolted to a wall. Restraint devices kept patients strapped to their beds, toilet bowls, and in otherwise thoroughly empty rooms. Bars made certain that those patients not restrained did not stray from their quarters, while fences surrounding the facility ensured that residents who were occasionally permitted to be outside did not leave the school to interact with Grafton's 6,000 citizens.[276]

The state's refusal to spend money on the Grafton State Home ultimately cost it money. North Dakota spent a mere $22/day on the care of Grafton State School's residents. Only Mississippi with an expenditure of $21.20/day fell below. Due to the parsimony with which the state legislature treated the facility, it often did not qualify for federal aid, resulting in the state carrying the entire financial load for the facility, rather than sharing it with the federal government.[277]

In 1980, ARC of North Dakota determined to file a lawsuit against the state for appropriating a million dollars for the construction of a swimming pool at Grafton's sister institution San Haven. While ostensibly for the residents of San Haven, a former tuberculosis hospital that now housed the most profoundly disabled of North Dakota's residents, ARC members knew that since patients could not leave the grounds of the facility, it was in actuality a pool for the community. It also pointed to the fact that the state, by putting forth the money, clearly intended to maintain San Haven. Twenty-three-year-old attorney Mike Williams represented ARC.[278]

In his videotaped exploration of the facilities, Williams gathered sufficient evidence to support literally hundreds of federal violations. The buildings stank of urine and feces, patients sat or lay in dirty diapers for hours, and bored residents frequently pounded their heads or hands against walls, ultimately requiring bandaging. Other patients clearly did not belong in the institutions, but rather remained there so as not to be a "burden" to society at large.[279]

Initially filed in the closing days of Governor Link's administration, Attorney General Allen Olson successfully argued for a delay, not realizing that during the intervening months, he would become governor and face the court case as one of his most trying experiences. When matters finally got to hand, the newly elected Attorney General Robert Wefald led the state's case. Wefald rejected suggestions by ARC that the case be settled via the employment of more attendants at the facilities, as well as the addition of at least $2 million to their budgets. He had been requested to do so by Olson and House Majority Leader Earl Strinden as they believed the suit usurped legislative authority.[280]

On January 28, 1982, *ARC v. ND* commenced in U.S. District Court in Bismarck before the honorable Judge Bruce Van Sickle. In the lawsuit as ultimately filed, ARC requested not only that the facility hire more attendants, but that they be appropriately trained to administer medicines, that medicines be given for illnesses and chronic conditions, not simply as chemical restraints, and that residents be provided proper dental, medical, and vision care. Moreover, the suit asked that regularly scheduled activities be planned for residents that they be allowed to practice the religion of their choice, that they be allowed to vote, and that they have appropriate clothing. As well, ARC requested air-conditioning, privacy, and fire safety for the residents. The facility, according to ARC, denied its residents basic civil rights.[281]

The state admitted that problems existed at Grafton and San Haven, but argued that funds did not, and hence obviated its responsibility to the residents. Judge Van Sickle hearing the admission of responsibility by the state, ruled in favor of the plaintiffs, declaring substandard conditions be rectified. During the remedy portion of the trial, besides ordering compliance with ARC's requests, the judge ordered San Haven closed and that the number of individuals living at Grafton radically be reduced. He urged the movement of individuals to community homes scattered across the state.[282]

If the ARC case provided Olson with headaches, so did a simple grain farmer: Gordon Kahl. Kahl associated himself with the Posse Comitatus, a right-wing extremist group that holds that the individual is sovereign and need not obey laws contrary to the Articles of Confederation, Perpetual, sourced from the Bible. If needed, Posse members hold the right to execute those who stand in the way of a Christian republic, particularly Jews who have formed a conspiracy to destroy the United States. In an effort to right the United States, members believe they should not pay income tax, send their children to public schools, or hold any government-issued document: driver's licenses, birth certificates, Social Security cards. Women, minorities, and Jews are accorded no rights in the Posse Comitatus with all power held in Christian grand juries.[283]

When Kahl refused to pay his taxes, and publicly made a show of not doing so, he attracted a following of the disenchanted throughout the Midwest-Great Plains, including several farmers in the Heaton and Medina areas of North Dakota. Kahl's theory, which gained the attention of farmers in distress, held that if the federal government could afford to send literally billions of dollars to support the state of Israel, but not aid its own farmers, the Jewish conspiracy had without doubt taken over the reins of power in the United States. His theories, as well as those of other Christian Identity movements, gained the support of a subset of troubled farmers, unable to see their way out of the economic stresses brought upon them by the agricultural crisis of the 1980s.[284]

His public declarations, as well as an outstanding warrant from a stay in federal prison after which he was to pay his income taxes, led the United States Marshal Service to attempt an arrest of Kahl and his immediate followers on Sunday, February 13, 1983, after a long and divisive meeting of the Posse in Medina. In a series of errors regarding the physical process—insufficient law enforcement numbers, last-minute planning, a poorly selected area for the arrest attempt, and so on—two federal marshals died, another was seriously injured and another with minor injuries. Kahl's son Yorie sustained serious injuries as well.[285]

A nationwide manhunt ensued, ultimately locating Kahl in an Identity compound in Arkansas. On June 3, 1983, following tear gas, flames, and gun fire, the badly burned body of Kahl and a local law enforcement officer were removed from the home of his protectors. His son Yorie, as well as Scott Faul, one of Kahl's adherents will spend the remainder of their lives in federal custody, while another of his followers spent ten years in prison for his role in the Medina shoot-out.[286] While not directly associated with the farm crisis of the decade, the willingness of so many in the state to publicly, or privately, adopt such radical beliefs with such unlikely culprits illustrated a serious force upon the plains as well as a symbol of frustration.

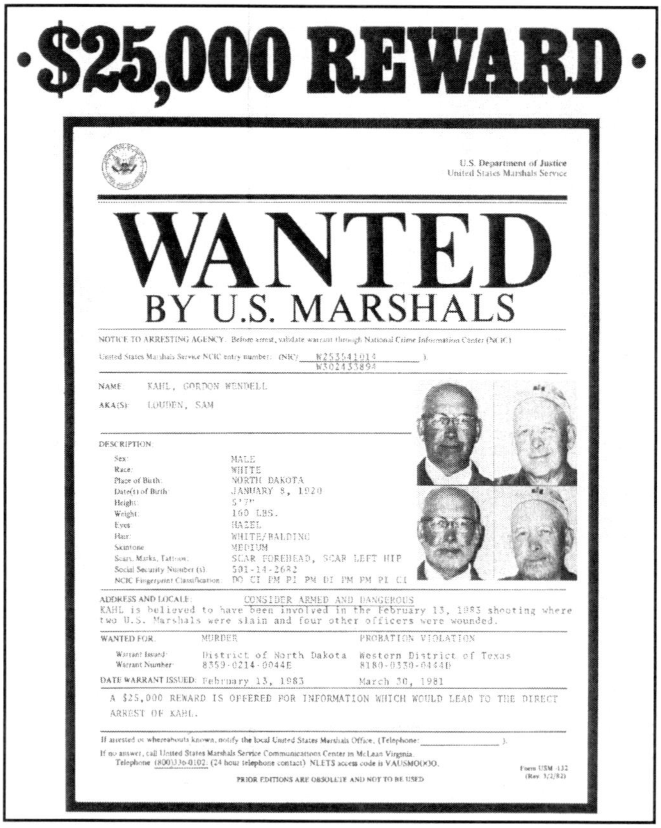

Gordon Kahl Wanted Poster, 1983

U.S. Marshal Service

People themselves became less and less a force upon the plains and prairies of the state. Census figures revealed that while the state as a whole grew during the first half of the 1980s, not all parts of the state grew at an equal pace. For example, census estimates from 1980 to 1984 illustrate a growth of approximately 28,000 residents; those individuals did not claim all parts of the state home in equal proportions. Indeed, the state's rural areas continued their decline, while its urban areas continued their growth. In consideration of the population variations, the fourteen counties of the slope region—that land beyond the Missouri River—only two counties gained population: Sioux, home of Standing Rock Reservation, and Mercer, home of considerable lignite mining and energy production.[287]

Growing counties and communities tended to already be centers of growth with major opportunities available in the form of governmental or industrial positions, or educational opportunities. For example, Burleigh County, home of the state capital grew, as did Cass and Grand Forks counties, also homes of governmental positions, both state and federal. Burleigh, Cass, and Grand Forks counties, as well as Stark County, could also claim growth, potentially as the result of being home to state universities. Sioux and

Rolette counties also claimed population increases, potentially due to the fact that they contained Indian Reservations.[288]

More and more individuals, however, were making their livings from industrial production. While industrial opportunities had existed in North Dakota from before its inception as a state, more and more opportunities arose as its first century drew to a close. As previously noted, coal and energy production provided a significant number of jobs in the west and west central portions of the state, as did oil production. Indeed, over the first years of the 1980s, oil production rose to 52.7 million barrels (1984), from a mere 24.8 million barrels in 1979.[289]

Elsewhere in the state, laborers could find quality employment in Gwinner, manufacturing Bobcat skid steers; in Hebron, producing bricks; in Pembina, working for Motor Coach Industries; or in Fargo, turning out Steiger tractors. Much of North Dakota's manufacturing was directly related to its agricultural production. In Drayton and Hillsboro, sugar beets became sugar; in West Fargo, steers became beef; in Fargo, sunflowers were processed into assorted products; while in Hatton, pinto beans were processed for human consumption. Elsewhere in the state, Roman Meal bread, mustard, and pasta flowed from the products of the state's soil. In total, far more individuals worked in the assorted branches of manufacturing than in agriculture.[290]

Bobcat skid steer manufactured at Gwinner, North Dakota

Courtesy of Joe Keller

American Crystal Sugar, Drayton

Courtesy, American Crystal Sugar Company.

More individuals found work in the tourism industry than ever before as well as the 1980s came along. Indeed, it was the state's third largest industry in the state by the start of the decade. Individuals could enjoy the recently reconstructed Medora to take in the musicals and tour the home of the Marquis de Mores, and walk the streets of a town where Theodore Roosevelt became a man.

Chateau de Mores at Medora

North Dakota Tourism/Bruce Wendt

International Peace Garden
North Dakota Tourism/Ren Davis

They could also take in the world-famous International Peace Garden; enjoy Native American festivals, as well as European-oriented ethnic festivals. Moreover, state parks abounded, as did small-scale museums and summer celebrations. Perhaps of even greater interest to North Dakotans as the 1980s began was the opening of the North Dakota Heritage Center in Bismarck in 1981.[291]

Nineteen eighty-one did not only mark the opening of the Heritage Center. It also marked the first time that most North Dakotans could legally gamble, albeit for small stakes and for the general benefit of charitable institutions. From its creation as a state, North Dakotans stood firm against the creation of a lottery or other gaming opportunities. Indeed, the first amendment to the constitution of North Dakota specifically banned lotteries and all forms of gift enterprises. However, by 1976, some minds considered the ban to be outdated and the constitution was again amended, this time to allow certain forms of charitable gaming.[292]

As first allowed in 1977, charitable gaming "authorize[d] bona fide nonprofit veterans', charitable, educational, religious, or fraternal organizations, civic and service clubs; or such other public-spirited organizations as it may recognize to conduct games of change when the entire net proceeds of the games [were] devoted to educational, patriotic, fraternal, religious or other public-spirited use." As Governor Link later recalled, the change in the constitution simply made legal the "smokers" that men's clubs had been holding for years, as well as the bingo games frequently held by Catholics. Link, himself opposed to any form of legalized gambling, allowed the bill to pass into law without his signature.[293]

As written, the law would permit small stakes gambling, initially limiting bets to $2, with the proceeds going to charitable institutions such as the Association for Retarded Citizens (ARC), Prairie Public Television, North Dakota Diabetes Association, and so on. A 1982 initiated measure to place limits upon even the limited charitable gaming failed to gain enough support to pass into law. A measure limiting nuclear developments, weaponry, and waste facilities did, however, clear the hurdle and become law that year.[294]

Beyond nuclear prohibitions and failed limitations on charitable gaming, the election of 1982 provided only a modicum of entertainment. Without a presidential or gubernatorial race to focus upon, the greatest attention fell on the congressional races. However, those did not provide a great deal of uncertainty. Democrat Quentin N. Burdick handily defeated Republican challenger Gene Knorr, 164,873 to 89,304, to commence his fourth complete term of office as a United States senator. And Byron Dorgan, also a Democrat, easily defeated his Republican opponent Kent Jones, 186,534 to 72,241, to start his second term as a member of the United States House of Representatives. If any surprise was to be found in the election returns, it came on the state level. For the first time in 16 years, the Democrats controlled the North Dakota House of Representatives. Also taking their place in the House and the Senate were 18 women legislators.[295]

In 1984, with the farm crisis becoming ever-more apparent to the citizens of North Dakota, the residents sought change. Indeed, a great deal of frustration seemed to center on Governor Olson, albeit in retrospect it would appear that there was little he could have done on a state level to staunch the pain of the farm crisis or to build the state's extractive industries or manufacturing at any greater pace. Nor, of course, did he seem to have the solution to the continuing exodus of North Dakotans to greener pastures in distant states.

The gubernatorial race pitted Olson, seeking his second term, versus Democrat-NPL candidate George A. Sinner. Sinner, with his farming background, served as president of the Red River Valley Sugarbeet Growers Association Board from 1975 to 1979, and as a member of the State Board of Higher Education. As his running mate, Sinner chose Ruth Meiers, the first woman to run for (and attain) the position of lieutenant governor in North Dakota. The campaign turned contentious as Olson struggled to put the best face on a difficult four years. When the counting was done, George Sinner had been elected the 29th governor of North Dakota, 173,922 to 140,460 for Olson. In a strange turn of events, Olson initially refused to relinquish the office of the governor. Olson maintained that he had been elected to a four-year term of office and therefore did not need to vacate his office until January 6, 1985, four years after his own term had begun. Sinner held that the term officially began on January 1, 1985. North Dakota's Supreme Court upheld Sinner's position on January 5, just one day prior to the date Olson initially intended to leave office. Sinner's term retroactively started January 1, 1985. In an initiated measure, voters affirmed their right to bear arms.[296]

Voters also affirmed their support of the Reagan Revolution by their votes that November. Reagan handily carried the state, 200,336 to 104,429 for the Democratic ticket of Walter Mondale and Geraldine Ferraro, the first woman to stand for the vice presidency of the United States. Mondale's status as a neighbor from Minnesota apparently carried no weight with voters. And, Byron Dorgan easily defeated his Republican challenger for his third term as sole United States representative from North Dakota.[297]

The first portion of the 1980s had been a difficult one for North Dakota: mild drought, farm crisis beyond the wildest of imagined fears, a lawsuit against the state that severely tarnished its image, continued out-migration, and oil prices that did not seem to meet the challenges of OPEC's power. As Sinner took the oath of office, he, and all North Dakotans, could only hope that the latter half of the decade would prove better than the first.

chapter 7

THE CRISIS CONTINUES
The Latter 1980s

The inauguration of a new governor did not dramatically alter the troubled economic conditions facing North Dakota's farmers. The agricultural sector would remain a serious drag upon the state's economy well into the next decade. The state did, however, reap the benefit of an improving market for oil, as well as one for electrical energy. Additionally, opportunities in manufacturing expanded, broadening the state's economic base. If this were not enough to celebrate, its citizenry heralded the arrival of North Dakota's second century as a state during George Sinner's governorship. Still the state's single largest economic sector ailed, making the remainder of the state restive, reliant as it was upon the toil of farmers and ranchers.

If anything, conditions for farmers worsened during the initial Sinner years. The problems, however, ran far deeper than he had the opportunity to correct. In part, problems arose from newly instituted measures from the federal government. In 1986, Reagan administration slashed dairy-production programs from the budget and placed strong limitations upon disaster payments and program benefits to individual farmers. In addition, the federal government froze commodity price supports and promised further reductions by 1987. Those farmers who benefited from Reagan's farm policy tended to be those with larger farm operations. Individual farmers and ranchers who ranked in the top 20 percent in terms of size of operation received slightly over 90 percent of all government subsidies to agriculture.[298]

Moreover, the base problems that started the farm crisis of the early 1980s remained firmly in place. Farmers simply owed too much money to local banking facilities and at exceptional rates of interest on depreciating land to ever completely free themselves from debt. Foreclosures meant not only anger and frustration, but also fewer farms and ranches, as well as fewer farmers and ranchers. Over the course of the latter 1980s, North Dakota lost approximately 2,000 farmers and ranchers, with 6,500 leaving agricultural pursuits over the entirety of the decade. Farm and ranch size increased only marginally, from 1,203 acres per unit in 1985 to 1,209 in 1989. Over this same period, nearly a half million acres fell out of production and became part of "urban" North Dakota: housing developments, airports, manufacturing sites, and so on.[299]

As a symbol of the farm crisis, the price of land continued to drop over the latter 1980s. There seemed little purpose in borrowing inflated dollars to produce crops that markets could not absorb. All throughout the state prices fell. In the northern Red River Valley, land that had sold for $643/acre in 1985 brought only $551 in 1989, while in the southern end of the valley, land that once sold for $730/acre now fetched $674. Similar conditions prevailed across the state. In the central region, prices dropped anywhere from $40 to $60/acre. Even grazing land saw a decline. Land that in 1985 sold for $203/acre in northwestern North Dakota now sold for $185/acre, while land in the slope dropped from $215/acre in 1985 to $169/acre in 1989.[300]

An examination of those individuals selling their land in the middle 1980s illustrates the depth of the farm crisis. While one might expect that farmers and ranchers in their 60s and 70s would be selling their land preparatory to retirement, the statistics revealed a somewhat different picture. In 1985 and 1986, the average age of farm/ranch sellers was below 55 years of age. Jerome Johnson, a professor of Agricultural Economics at North Dakota State University, suggested that "financial pressures, debts and foreclosures appeared to be the leading reasons" for land sales in the latter half of the 1980s. Buyers during this troubled time generally proved to be farmers or ranchers who already held extensive properties and usually were over age 55. Younger buyers often failed to find sufficient capital to enter into agriculture in the 1980s or often had been dissuaded from the decision by their parents and grandparents.[301]

North Dakota's farmers were not aided in their quest for success by commodity markets. Corn, for example, sold for $2.63/bushel in 1984, dropped to $1.50/bushel in 1986, before rising to $2.36/bushel at the close of the decade. Similarly, soybean prices dropped, and then rose again over the closing years of the decade. In 1985, for example, beans sold for $5.05/bushel, falling to $4.78/bushel in 1986, only to rise to $5.69/bushel in 1989. Sunflowers responded somewhat differently to the crisis of the 1980s. In 1985, sunflowers sold for $7.93/cwt., falling to $6.90/cwt. in 1986, but rising to the $12.90/cwt. in 1989.[302]

North Dakota's wheat prices tracked quite similarly to that of sunflowers. Undifferentiated wheat sold for $3.08/bushel in 1985, falling to $2.42/bushel the following year, only to rise again to $3.72/bushel in 1989. Durum, the state's ultimate cash crop, wavered as well over the latter 1980s. In 1985, durum sold for $3.22/bushel, falling to $2.70/bushel in 1986, only to climb to $4.70/bushel in 1988, and fall again in 1989 to $3.46/bushel. Sugar beets, supported in part by federal subsidy dollars, steadily increased in value over the latter 1980s. While in 1985, a ton of beets sold for $33.80, by 1989 that same ton drew $42.10.[303]

Beef producers fared much better than grain farmers in the 1980s. Indeed, throughout the 1980s, the price of beef rose dramatically. In 1985, a fat steer brought $58.34/cwt. By 1984, he brought $64.61/cwt., and by the close of the decade, he brought a whopping $72.52/cwt.[304]

Throughout the course of the 1980s, farmers and ranchers sought a variety of methods to improve their economic condition. While for some this meant selling the family holdings and finding work in an urban environment, others determined to stay on the land and augment their incomes via new, and, oft times, untried mechanisms, but also old, albeit modified methods.

Cooperative marketing endeavors, popular since before the turn of the twentieth century, took on new significance as farmers attempted to cut out the middleman in the process of moving their products from farms and ranches to the ultimate consumer.

Grain cooperatives, frequently organized by agencies such as the Farmers' Union, or an alternative organization of farmers, had dotted the landscape for generations in the form of their massive elevators and storage facilities. However, as the conditions for farmers and ranchers worsened during the 1980s, new cooperatives devoted to new products came to North Dakota.

Throughout the 1980s, cooperatives devoted to the marketing of bison meat, potatoes, wheat, barley, lignite, dry edible beans, strawboard, beef, and carrots all operated in North Dakota. While some, such as sugar, dated to the decades prior to the crisis years of the 1980s, most did not. In the latter 1980s and early 1990s, over three hundred different cooperatives operated in North Dakota. This number included a few electric and telephone cooperative operations, but generally focused on agricultural marketing. Per capita, North Dakotans engaged in more cooperative endeavors than any other state.[305]

Not all farmers turned to cooperatives to weather the economic storm. Others, particularly those located in the central and western portions of the state, turned their land into private hunting preserves, allowing only those individuals who paid the right to hunt upon their land. While some cried foul with regard to the freedom to hunt unfettered, or with regard to unfair advantages offered to well-to-do out-of-state hunters, and still others protested the "captive" nature of the hunt, the funds supplied by such enterprises cannot be overlooked in ranchers' efforts to stay afloat.[306]

Other ranchers, and to some extent farmers, offered urban dwellers the opportunity to spend a weekend or even a week on an operating ranch, far away from their busy city lives. From rustic experiences in bunkhouses to elegant bed-and-breakfasts, catering to the needs of vacationers became a part of the rural economy. Indeed, during the 1980s, and continuing to this day, agri-tourism has become a significant factor in the farm economy. As an example, in the early 1980s, the John and Jennifer Hanson family of Bowman felt the pressures of the farm crisis. John Hanson initially attempted his hand at selling sawn ponderosa pine from the ranch to improve his revenue stream. To house his equipment and serve as a shop for his sawmill, Hanson built a rough-hewn cabin. Even before the cabin was completed, Hanson had individuals lining up to rent it. The North Dakota Department of Tourism encouraged Hanson to build additional cabins, noting that no guest ranch yet existed in western North Dakota. He built two additional guest cabins by 1986, electrifying and adding running water to each as time and finances allowed. His Logging Camp Ranch also profited from the sales of bison meat and from bison hunts arranged for paying guests.[307]

Other farmers turned to organic enterprises in their efforts to save the family farm. Terry and Janet Jacobson of Wales, North Dakota, determined to tap the natural foods market in order to diversify their offerings, and more importantly, to weather significant market fluctuations. Along the way, they turned to producing organically grown sunflowers, wheat, oats, millets, and alfalfa on their section farm. In addition, they cast their attention to raising hormone-free, grass-fed beef and sheep. Besides their value as meat, the sheep were also shorn, with their wool turned into yarn, felt, or specialized clothing and crafts sold only through art galleries.[308] While some farmers could not see past the woes of the 1980s or were indebted too far to reasonably recover, others made lemonade from the proverbial lemons handed them by the farm economy.

Despite the best efforts of the most innovative farmers, the natural environment did not always cooperate with their plans and their toil. From 1988 through 1992, the state as a whole suffered from conditions nearly as bad as those endured during the Dust Bowl era of the 1930s. Farmers and ranchers faced difficulties in maintaining pastures for grazing their livestock and ponds and streams for watering their animals, as well as sufficient soil moisture to raise crops. Accordingly, livestock on North Dakota's farms and ranches declined, and crop yields decreased, particularly on formerly irrigated acres.[309]

While farmers and ranchers perhaps bore the brunt of the drought, municipalities as well as their residents felt the power of the natural environment from those dreadful years as well. Municipal water supplies dwindled to the point of restrictions being placed upon lawn sprinkling and other high-use activities. Moreover, recreation in the state declined, directly impacting its purveyors. With fire danger dramatically increased, camping and picnicking declined. Similarly, with reduced water flow and depth, fish and wildlife dwindled, as did the sportsmen who sought them. The economic impact of the drought could not be measured by any extant methods; the event was simply too all encompassing to be calculated in its impact on the state's economy.[310]

As if to mock the horrors of the drought, the eastern portion of North Dakota underwent significant flooding in the spring of 1989. From Wahpeton in the south to Fargo and Grand Forks in the central Red River Valley, cities struggled to contain the floodwaters of the Red. North of Grand Forks, the danger dissipated somewhat as slower melting conditions and a relatively low flowing tributary in the form of the Red Lake River, served to lessen the threat of flooding. Bob Simons, Grand Forks city assessor, estimated that the flood cost the community approximately $730,000.[311]

Harsh weather and poor economic conditions on the farms and ranches of the state served to dampen the increase in population recorded by the 1980 decennial census. While the 1980 census counted approximately 652,000 residents and later censuses of the decade placed the state's population at approximately 680,000 in 1984, the gains could not be maintained. Declining economic conditions took their toll over the remaining years of the decade. In 1985, the estimated population fell to 676,000, falling to 661,000 in 1987 and to 646,000 by 1989.[312]

As in previous years, rural western counties saw the greatest drop in population as their residents moved to urban areas in the state, or even left the state entirely in search of the proverbial and literal greener pastures. Some counties—Cass, Grand Forks, and Burleigh—registered growth over the decade. However, even as former rural dwellers moved to these communities, the overall outlook dimmed with the knowledge that more individuals were leaving the state than just moving around within it.[313]

Demographers noted several disturbing trends beyond the fact of rural depopulation in their investigations of North Dakota. One of particular note involved the out-migration of young adults. With a significant loss of residents in their 20s and early 30s to other states, North Dakota faced a problem of considerable proportions. Not only did the individuals leave the state, but so did their children, as well as their children yet unborn. Not only did this portend a declining population, but also a looming impact on education, churches, and businesses inclined to youths, and also upon the general "human capital" required to infuse communities and governments with new perspectives.[314]

Paralleling the disturbing decline in young adults came the concomitant incline in the proportion of the elderly. While only an approximate 13.5 percent of the state's population was over the age of 65, the ramifications of this could not be ignored. An aging population meant that additional resources would need to be directed towards the needs and care of the elderly. Often this would be magnified by the absence of the elders' children and grandchildren who had left the state in search of better economic opportunities. Compounding the problem was the frequent closure of facilities and businesses important to the elderly as the out-migration of youth took place, particularly in rural regions; health care facilities, churches, small town grocery stores, cafés, and other businesses shuttered in the absence of a youthful population. Even the young required to staff nursing homes became harder to locate. The number of individuals 85 and older increased significantly over the 1980s, making North Dakota the state with the highest proportion of the truly elderly.[315]

Knowledge of such demographic shifts caused a stir not only in North Dakota, but in places far distant, specifically New Jersey. After studying the Great Plains for a number of years, Dr. Frank J. Popper, a professor at Rutgers University, along with Dr. Deborah Epstein Popper, his wife and also a professor at Rutgers, declared that a considerable proportion of the nation's midland should never have been settled by European American homesteaders. The harsh climate, complete with blizzards, droughts, hot summers, bitter winters, frequent hail storms and tornadoes, as well as locusts and range fires, and short growing seasons allowed for the greatest "environmental miscalculation in American history." Within the next generation, the Poppers predicted, the region would "become almost totally depopulated."[316]

Following a quick and depressing history of the plains, somewhat selectively presented, the Poppers offered their solution to the "miscalculation." Given the region's "bleak future" due to water shortages, declining resource prices, shrinking social services, increasing bank failures, and rising farm foreclosures, they suggested that large portions of the Great Plains, including a significant portion of North Dakota, be returned to a "Buffalo Commons." The concept behind the commons was that the federal government should treat the Great Plains as a distinct region, something never before done, acknowledging its unsuitability for agricultural production.[317]

Rather, the federal government should intervene to deprivatize specific portions of the plains, allowing it to return to one large commons, an area devoid of permanent human inhabitation, where, among other things, the buffalo would return following the dismantling of human habitations, man-made structures and fences, and the replanting of shortgrass. Ultimately, depending in part on the wishes of Native Americans who once claimed the land, the identified regions would revert to "a vast land mass, largely empty and unexploited." The Buffalo Commons would reflect better land use and social policy for the Great Plains than at any time since the first European Americans claimed their 160 acres of privatized land.[318]

It is safe to say that the Poppers' plan did not receive positive acclaim on the Great Plains, North Dakota included. Many argued that the region, despite its sparse population, remained a vital part of the United States, producing beef and wheat, as well as providing oil and coal to the nation.

As suggested by the Poppers' detractors, coal and oil, as well as the production of electrical energy for state use, as well as for exportation, remained a vital part of the North Dakota economy. Despite a lagging economy and declining prices for crude oil in much of the 1980s, production remained significant. In 1985, North Dakotans pumped approximately 52 million barrels of oil from the western region of the state. Besides adding wealth to individuals, the 6.5 percent extraction tax added approximately $151 million to the state's coffers, although this declined to approximately $57 million dollars in 1989. An excess of oil production by Saudi Arabia flattened the market for North Dakota oil, and caused some financial distress to those in the western and northwestern portions of the state who had profited significantly in the mid-1980s.[319]

Lignite production remained a significant portion of the economy for western and central North Dakotans throughout the 1980s, rising over the course of the 1980s from 11 million tons to 29 million tons at the close of the decade. The growth in lignite mining came even as competition rose from coal banks in Wyoming and Montana. The majority of lignite mined in the state, estimated from 80 to 85 percent, remained in the state, generally used for the production of electrical energy, which in turn was often exported to other regions of the nation.[320]

Throughout the majority of the 1980s, three electrical companies operated in North Dakota: Basin Electric, Minnkota Power Cooperative, and Great River Energy. For the most part, the generating plants operated in North Dakota's coal fields, limiting the need for transportation and presumptively providing greater returns for their investors. Plants produced electricity at Beulah, Center, Underwood, and Stanton.[321]

Beyond the sales of lignite enriching individuals and corporations, they also helped to fill the state's coffers. In the 1986–87 biennium, the coal severance tax yielded $52,558,231, while the coal conversion tax yielded $20,775,998, reflecting the production of 39,490,609,110 kilowatt hours of electricity.[322]

Of particular interest to North Dakotans, as well as those fearing continued energy shortages was the coal gasification plant near Beulah. The plant had commenced construction in 1981, becoming operational in 1984. Construction expenses rose astronomically beyond their initial $600 million estimate to over $2 billion. As originally designed, the plant would on a daily basis convert 14,000 tons of lignite into 125 million cubic feet of substitute natural gas. The nation's first synthetic gas plant, however, failed. Natural gas prices dropped and the American Natural Gas Company and its subsidiary the Michigan-Wisconsin Pipeline Company defaulted on the loan with the United States government claiming the plant in August 1985.[323]

Dakota Gasification, Great Plains Synfuels Plant, Beulah

Courtesy of Basin Electric Power Cooperative

Basin Electric, through its for-profit subsidiary, Dakota Gasification Company, purchased the plant from the federal government in October 1, 1988, naming its operation the Great Plains Synfuels Plant. In its current iteration, it uses 18,000 tons of lignite daily to produce 160 million cubic feet of "natural" gas. Its by-products are used broadly and included in the manufacture of agricultural fertilizer, specialty lighting gases, carbon dioxide, resins, benzene, liquid nitrogen, pesticides, and antioxidants.[324]

The election of 1986, proved illustrative of the crises of the general economy. Not only did agriculture and oil see hard times, but so did several major businesses in the state. Steiger (tractors), Gold Seal (household cleaning products), and Great Plains (computer software) were all forced to reorganize. Such economic factors bred discontent among the state's residents and despite it being neither a gubernatorial or presidential election year, North Dakotans turned out in record numbers to cast their ballots. Some 295,277 individuals cast ballots in 1986, surpassed to date only by the presidential election years of 1972 and 1980. In a surprise turn of events, Republican Mark Andrews lost his bid for reelection as United States senator. Taking his place, by the slimmest of margins, was Kent Conrad, Democrat and formerly state tax commissioner. Byron Dorgan retained his seat in the United States House of Representatives, nearly trebling the votes gained by his Republican competitor.[325]

Besides electing officials to office, voters in 1986 also weighed in on a series of constitutional issues. Perhaps reflecting on the difficulties of Sinner physically taking office from Olson, the citizenry voted to make December 15 the official start to gubernatorial terms. They also voted to prohibit a state lottery, and to keep stores closed on Sunday, even after noon.[326]

Representative (now Senator) Kent Conrad

Photo courtesy of Senator Kent Conrad.

In a time of crisis, the state turned to the Democratic Party as never before. Indeed, for the first time in the state's history Democrats held the state senate. Moreover, all of the state's federal representatives were Democrats, as were the state treasurer and the attorney general. Twenty women held seats in the state legislature, more than at any previous time. Beryl Levine, the first woman to serve on the North Dakota Supreme Court, had taken office only one year prior. Unfortunately, the state's first woman lieutenant governor, Ruth Meiers, became seriously ill with cancer. Her duties curtailed, she died in 1987. Upon her passing, Lloyd Omhdahl, a Democrat from Grand Forks, was appointed to fill the position until the 1988 election.[327]

North Dakota Supreme Court Justice Beryl Levine

Supreme Court of North Dakota

The election of 1988 did not provide the surprises of the previous one. George Sinner again stood for governor, with Lloyd Omdahl as his lieutenant governor. Facing Republican challenger Leon L. Mallberg, he handily defeated his competition with a 60,000 vote margin. Quentin Burdick, despite being in his 80th year, easily defeated Republican Earl Strinden, former House Majority Leader, by nearly the same margin. Byron Dorgan also retained his seat in the United States House of Representatives, gathering 212,583 votes to his Republican competitor's 84,475. Moreover in a repeat of the 1986 election, North Dakotans turned down a state-operated lottery.[328]

Given North Dakota's track record with regard to presidential elections, the results of George H. W. Bush, Republican, versus Michael Dukakis, Democrat, came as no surprise. Bush claimed the votes of 166,559 voters, while Dukakis claimed 127,739.[329]

Although not directly tied to the election, another event occurred in 1988, changing the face of North Dakota, as well as many other states, for decades to come. In 1988, the federal government passed into law the Indian Gaming Regulatory Act. In essence, the federal government discerned that tribal governments, as separate political entities, could enter into gambling operations for the general public's entertainment. Indeed, as separate entities, a number of tribes across the United States had already opened casinos as a means of generating income for their people. In the process of passing the Indian Gaming Act, the Congress codified the rights of tribal populations to conduct gambling enterprises on their own land. The law passed Congress in part due to its capacity to build tribal self-sufficiency, economic development, and viable native governmental structures. It also was intended to provide the participating tribes some sort of financial protection from professional gaming management companies, as well as to generally oversee the regulation of gambling and the rise in crime often associated with gambling institutions.[330]

Indian gaming in North Dakota would need to await the next decade.

Indian casinos made a significant impact on tourism at their first arrival in the early 1990s. However, even before gaming, tourism gained ground in terms of its economic impact on the state. In the closing years of the 1980s, tourism regularly brought nearly $300 million per year into the state. Prime tourist attractions included Medora, the newly opened Heritage Center in Bismarck, the International Peace Gardens, the state's numerous historic sites, Knife River National Park, the confluence of the Missouri and Yellowstone Rivers, and pretty much anything associated with the Lewis and Clark Expedition of 1804–06. Of course, the great outdoors also called visitors to North Dakota for hunting and fishing opportunities, farm-oriented vacations, water sports on Lake Sakakawea, and hiking through the Badlands.[331]

Medora Musical, Medora

North Dakota Tourism/Jason Lindsey

Badlands

Courtesy of Dr. James Walla

Lake Sakakawea

© Chuck Haney

Industrial concerns made their contributions to the state's economy as well. Throughout the closing years of the decade, manufacturing firms, excluding energy production, contributed approximately $634 million per annum to the state's finances. Firms manufactured or processed tractors, skid steers, bricks, pasta, beef and bison meat, computer software applications, airplanes and airplane parts, agricultural equipment, ethanol, frozen potato and bread products, as well as containers, and finished wood products.[332]

On November 2, 1889, North Dakota became the 39th state to join the union. Having survived the numerous hazards of statehood—drought, flooding, poor economic times, political infighting, and so on—warranted celebrating in 1989. Accordingly, planning well in advance, in 1981 the state legislature appointed the seven-member North Dakota Centennial Commission. The legislature reestablished this commission in 1983 with a sunset clause of June 30, 1991. Funded by a state allowance of $10,000, as well as by donations, grants, and bequests, former Governor Arthur Link accepted the chairmanship at the request of Governor George Sinner.[333]

In an effort to involve as many of the state's residents as possible, the festivities took place over a four-year span, and included as many communities as possible. Communities throughout the state were encouraged to develop their own celebratory plans: planting a garden, improving a park, holding a parade, or simply undertaking a community project to improve their home town. Jamestown held "Division Day" to commemorate the decision to create two separate states from Dakota Territory; Bismarck celebrated the Enabling Act, which allowed the future states of North and South Dakota to call constitutional conventions; Dickinson and New Rockford hosted Founders Day to commemorate the election of delegates to the constitutional convention; President George H. W. Bush planted a tree on the capitol grounds, marking the first visit from a sitting president to the state in nearly three decades; and Minot celebrated Citizens Day, to commemorate the vote of North Dakota's white, male citizenry to accept the constitution as prepared. Individuals throughout the state were encouraged to plant 100 million trees by 2000.[334]

The largest event of all came on July 4, 1989, commemorating the day that the constitutional conventioneers met in Bismarck one hundred years before to begin writing the state's first (and only) constitution. The day began with Native American dancing and singing, followed by addresses from the state's congressional delegation, Governor Sinner, members of the Supreme Court, and assorted state legislators. Between speeches, morning attendees of the festivities could hear the Centennial Band, the Centennial Choir, David Solheim as the Centennial Poet, and Chuck Suchy as the Centennial Troubadour. Later, a parade drew tens of thousands to Mandan to hear the Centennial Band, to see floats from 80 communities and nearly 250 other institutions, as well as over 500 horses and dozens of covered wagons that had traveled from all points in the state.[335]

Although the day scorched the already dry earth, topping out at 104 degrees shortly after noon, North Dakotans remained enthused, clustered around the capitol grounds. They listened to Bobby Vee, Myron Floren, Roy Clark, and the comedy team of Williams and Ree. As dark approached, a laser light show, set to patriotic music, flashed against the side of the 18-story capitol. As night fell, over 160,000 individuals packed the capitol grounds awaiting the promised fireworks. And as the sky lit up, North Dakotans could reflect on a century of statehood and only wonder as to what the second century would bring.[336]

The inaugural decade of that second century would provide partial answers, at least with regard to population, politics, economics, and the environment.

chapter 8

WAITING FOR THE GOOD TIMES
The Early 1990s

As it has every ten years since the founding of the republic, the nation called for a census of its people in 1990, seeking to know not only their number, but their general occupation, their race, their dwelling places, and their family structure, among other elements. With regard to North Dakota, some issues were surprising and some were anticipated.

Among the anticipated elements, given the continuing crisis in agriculture and the continuing drought that showed no signs of letting up, and the dreadfully low prices for the extractive industries of coal and oil, it came as no significant surprise that the state's population fell. In 1980, the state's population stood at 652,717. By 1990, the population dropped to 638,800, a drop of slightly more than two percent. As might be anticipated, the largest drops in population, by county, came from the western portion of the state: the regions hardest hit by the drought and decline in oil prices.[337]

Fourteen counties make up the region of North Dakota generally known as "the slope," the area bounded by the Missouri River, South Dakota and Montana. Only two of these counties, Sioux and Mercer, gained population over the decade, 1980-90. Sioux County, home of Standing Rock Indian Reservation, had the lowest median age of any county in the state, in essence meaning that more of its residents were of child-bearing age. Also gaining population was Mercer County, a region high in coal reserves, as well as the area of considerable electrical energy production.[338]

While some counties lost but a few individuals, Billings County for example declined by only 30 residents over the decade, other counties witnessed astounding drops in population. Hettinger County lost 830 residents, amounting to nearly 20 percent of its population; Slope County lost 22 percent of its population. Billings County had a median age of 33.5, while Hettinger's was 40.5, and Slope's was 34.8. In each case, the probability of further childbearing was relatively slight; meaning that only further decline in population stood on the horizon these counties.[339]

Counties gaining population over the course of the 1980s included Burleigh, Cass, Grand Forks, Mercer, Rolette and Sioux. Burleigh, Cass and Grand Forks counties hovered around 30 years of age for a median, as did Mercer. However, Sioux and Rolette counties, home of the Standing Rock Indian Reservation and Turtle Mountain Indian

Reservation, respectively, had relatively low median ages, 22.9 and 26.6, respectively. The chances for further grow appeared quite favorable in these counties.[340]

The population increases in Burleigh, Cass and Grand Forks counties did not appear so much to be a factor of natural increase, but as a reflection of individuals moving to the communities in search of social and economic opportunities, as well as educational ones in the cases of Cass and Grand Forks counties with their state universities.

With regard to median age, the census revealed other interesting points as well. Urban dwellers tended to be younger than their rural counterparts. Urban individuals with regard to median age averaged 29.9 years of age, while rural individuals averaged 35.8 years of age. All told, the drift from rural to urban, as well as the declining population of rural areas seemed destined to continue. As well, the 1990 census was the first to mark a dramatic passage for the state of North Dakota. For the first time, more individuals lived in urban areas, considered communities of at least 2,500, than lived in rural areas, those with less than 2,500 individuals. For a state holding on to a proud tradition of agricultural supremacy, the pill could only be considered a bitter one.[341]

In terms of its ethnicity and racial make-up, the 1990 census recorded changes as well. By the 1980 schedule of population, 625,557 individuals classified themselves as "white"; the census of 1990 recorded 604,142, a decline of approximately three percent, slightly exceeding the state's average decline of two percent. Conversely, the African American population rose over the course of the 1980s, albeit by a small margin. Whereas in 1980 2,568 African Americans called North Dakota home, by 1990, 3,524 did so, perhaps reflecting the growing number of individuals serving on the state's military bases, as well as attending its state universities.[342]

The population of Hispanic residents, regardless of origin rose slightly over the decade, climbing from 3,902 to 4,665. Moreover, the census of 1990 reflected the changing ethnicity of North Dakota's population. The enumerators catalogued individuals from China, Korea, Laos, Thailand, Fiji and Samoa. This list had been somewhat less extensive in the 1980 enumeration of North Dakota.[343]

Given North Dakota's expansive heritage of Native Americans, the increase in the number resident in the state proved somewhat interesting. In the census of 1980, the state enumerated 20,120 individuals of American Indian heritage, undifferentiated by specific tribe. In the census of 1990, greater specificity crept into the statistical analysis of population. While a total of 25,870 Native Americans claimed residency in North Dakota via self-determination and tribal standards, by no means did all of these individuals live on the state's reservations. Indeed, only 20,087 lived on the state's reservations. The remainder of those so enumerated lived throughout the state, but not on reservation lands. At Devils Lake Sioux Reservation, now Spirit Lake Indian Reservation, 3,588 Native Americans were enumerated. At Fort Berthold, 5,396 members of the Three Affiliated Tribes reported their presence, while in the North Dakota portion of the Standing Rock Reservation, 3,761 predominantly Sioux individuals declared themselves to be Native American. Elsewhere, the tiny portion of the Lake Traverse/Sisseton Reservation in North Dakota counted 237 individuals. And at Turtle Mountain Indian Reservation, including both the reservation and trust lands, 7,106 Ojibwa, Cree and Métis answered the enumerator's questions.[344]

Although the census did not record occupational category, as it had in 1980, farmers still played a major role in the state's economy. Despite their dwindling numbers and hard times, the single largest aspect of North Dakota's economy came from its rural sector. And that rural sector continued to ache as the 1980s turned into the 1990s. In 1960, 56,000 farmers and ranchers worked North Dakota's 42,100,000 agricultural acres, making for an average operation of 752 acres. In 1970, 45,500 farmers and ranchers toiled on 41,900,000 acres, providing for an average farm/ranch size of 921 acres. By 1980, the number of farmers and ranchers had dropped to 40,000, tending 41,700,000 acres, making an average-sized operation 1,042 acres. However, by 1990, the number of farmers and ranchers laboring on the state's agricultural lands had dropped to 33,500 on 490,500,000 acres for an average of 1,224 acres per operation.[345]

Scholars such as Osha Gray Davidson, *Broken Heartland: The Rise of American's Rural Ghetto*, decried the state of American agriculture over the last two generations. He saw that industrialized agriculture had made for larger and seemingly more efficient and cost-effective farms, but that along the way, sacrifices had been made which were too immense for the nation's well-being. Increased income for a powerful few farmers and ranchers, he believed, could not make up for the damage inflicted by toxic chemicals, monoculture production, dramatic soil erosion, and groundwater despoliation. Beyond the damage to the environment, he saw the quality of life in the nation's small community cultural centers deteriorating: schools closing, churches shuttering, small businesses selling out, an aging population, youth working at tasks beyond their age and skill level, and, ultimately, a loss of democracy.[346]

Not everyone, however, felt that the agricultural scene's changes came at the detriment of the American landscape. Writing in 2005, Dennis S. Nordin and Roy V. Scott, *From Prairie Farmer to Entrepreneur: The Transformation of Midwestern Agriculture*, could view the past with a bit more sanguinity. As they noted, memories of the good old days did not always reflect reality. Rather, quite frequently, the good old days had been ones of hardship and deprivation. Accordingly, then, to Nordin and Scott, "Whether by grand design, chance, or competition, the coinciding disappearance of and enlargement of farms have helped to make the North Central Region the global model of agricultural development.... Without these departures, better-skilled farmers could not have expanded their agricultural operations."[347]

Regardless of opinion on farming operations, grain prices remained relatively low during the early years of the 1990s. Corn, for example, sold for $2.28/bushel in 1990, less than it had averaged in 1974 ($3.02/bushel). Corn prices remained in the lower $2.00/bushel range throughout the 1990–94 period. Flax, a relative commercial newcomer to the agricultural scene in North Dakota, albeit one that had been raised in the earliest years of Dakota Territory's existence, sold for $5.27/bushel in 1990, but fell to $3.52/bushel the next year, returning to the $4.50/bushel range by 1994. Throughout the early 1990s, the price for soybeans remained relatively steady at approximately $5.50/bushel. Sunflowers were a bit more volatile in the 1990-94 period, rising to $10.40/cwt. in 1990 to $8.69/cwt. just one year later.[348]

Wheat, always North Dakota's prime crop, seemed unable to find and maintain a price in the early 1990s. Undifferentiated, it sold for $2.60/bushel in 1990, rising to $3.45/bushel by 1994. Durum prices, generally running a bit higher than spring wheat, trended higher in the 1990s. In 1990, a bushel of durum sold for $2.63/bushel, rising to $4.62/bushel in 1994. Sugar beets sold for approximately $40.00/ton throughout the 1990s. Beef prices ranged from a high of $77.40/cwt. in 1990 to a low of $68.67 in 1994.[349]

Farmland prices rose over the early 1990s, reflecting at least a minimal sense of optimism on the farm front. Land which had sold in the northern end of the Red River Valley in the late 1980s for approximately $550/acre, now sold for approximately $640/acre. Southern valley land rebounded from its late 1980s price of $674/acre to approximately $750/acre. Land prices, always lower in the western portion of the state where ranching prevailed, also rose in value, albeit slightly. Most land in the slope could be purchased for slightly over $200/acre, with some selling for as little as $149/acre.[350]

The problem, loosely stated, fell upon inflationary prices in the general economy, but deflationary prices in the realm of agriculture. While commodity prices remained steady, or even dropped somewhat, the inputs required to produce those commodities kept on the rise. Diesel fuel, herbicides, pesticides, agricultural equipment, irrigation equipment, veterinary services, and the like all rose, as did the basic accoutrements of living. Insurance, groceries, gasoline, electrical energy, clothing, medical care and the like all rose, resulting in poverty for far too many North Dakotans.

A 1992 study illustrated that 14.4 percent of North Dakotans lived in poverty, higher than the national average of 13.5 percent, as well as the North Dakota rate of 1980, 12.6 percent. Poverty could not be claimed as only an urban issue. Rather, one-third of all United States farm households fell below the poverty line. Even established farmers had difficulties making both ends meet. Twenty-three percent of long term farmers and their families lived below the poverty line in North Dakota in 1992.[351]

In an effort to maintain their lives on the farms and ranches of North Dakota, its agriculturalists tried a variety of means to achieve success. Former state senator Jim Kusler, Beulah, determined to turn his traditional beef operation into one focusing upon the production of certified organic beef, while Dean and Paula Swenson, Walcott, decided that their use of herbicides not only were expensive, but they also were a detriment to the soil. Accordingly, the Swensons turned to goat ranching as a method to control leafy spurge, an environmentally friendly response to an age-old pest, as well as a marketable product to the state's increasing numbers of Somali and Muslim residents. Others remained faithful to their cooperative endeavors in an attempt to profit from the land.[352]

Although still not the most popular people on the Great Plains, Drs. Frank and Deborah Epstein Popper gained adherents over the 1990s. Their Buffalo Commons theory of deprivatizing large portions of the Great Plains over the next twenty to thirty years which had been poorly received at its initial publication, gathered followers slowly, as their initial predictions came to pass. As they had suggested, with the decline in federal crop subsidies, the closing of bomber and missile bases as Cold War tensions eased, continued calls upon fast-falling aquifers, and the changing American diet, portions of the Plains, including sections of North Dakota fell below the six-person/square mile definition of "frontier".[353]

Professors Frank and Deborah Epstein Popper

Courtesy of Rutgers University, University Relations

University of North Dakota economist Dr. Lowell R. Goodman could see the validity of the Buffalo Commons theory, as expanded upon in *The Economic Health of North Dakota.* By his perceptions, the Buffalo Commons was coming to North Dakota of its own accord, no federal intervention required. Studying the population of North Dakota, its occupations, travel, shopping and consumption habits, as well as examining the changes modernity brought to agricultural production, left Goodman with a somewhat painful conclusion. If North Dakota wanted to maintain its youth, it would turn its focus upon eight urban points, and leave the remainder to suffer its demise.[354]

As Goodman saw it, Williston, Minot, Devils Lake, Grand Forks, Fargo, Jamestown, Mandan-Bismarck and Dickinson, as well as potentially Wahpeton, could all serve as growth centers for the state. Each of the designated communities would service an area from which drivers could access the town in an hour and a half of driving or less. These communities would serve as "growth poles" providing jobs, cultural opportunities, shopping, and services. The remainder of the state, while not deprivatized in the manner of the Poppers, would continue to lose population until a point below which the majority of individuals would choose not to live.[355]

For Goodman, the case for growth centers came naturally. As he noted in his concluding commentary, "From an economic point of view we're not doing as well as we could." Farms disappeared at a rate of 593 per year from 1974 to 1996; North Dakota's per capita personal income ranked 41st in the nation in 1993; total personal income in 1993 ranked the state 49th in the nation; and the state's economic growth rate was only slightly above half of that for the nation as a whole. With small towns dying as people drove for product selection, as well as pure entertainment to one of the major cities to purchase goods, the landscape of the state underwent significant change. Eventually the small stores in the small towns of North Dakota shuttered their windows and doors, leaving perilously few young men and women to produce and raise the next generation of small town bankers, store keepers and service professionals. With farm size growing and family size falling, schools shrunk and then consolidated. Ultimately, according to Goodman, "We [could not] lose sight of the main goal, keeping our young people in the state."[356]

Not everyone, however, was ready to count North Dakota or its residents out. Dr. Scot Arthur Stradley, also a University of North Dakota professor, examined the same conditions as Goodman and came to a completely variant conclusion. From his perspective, North Dakotans had weathered hard times in the past, and would most likely do so again. Aiding them in their recovery, according to Stradley, would be additional cooperative endeavors by farmers and value-added agriculturalists, as well as the recently instituted Indian gaming. As his theory went, farmers and investors should turn their attention to producing end-market products from their agricultural wares, i.e., meat from beef, pasta from durum, bread from spring wheat, etc. Via cooperative engagement, more money, leading to more jobs and more reasons for youth to remain in North Dakota, could be generated.[357]

Indian gaming also provided opportunity for growth according to Stradley's theorizing. With opportunities to gamble close to home, not only North Dakotans, but also Canadians and residents of nearby states would add to the state's economy, providing growth for the region's economically depressed reservations, and also adding to the number of Native American youth remaining in the state. Regardless of the theory embraced—Goodman's or Stradley's—maintaining population, particularly a youthful one became central to the concerns of state leaders, economists and business interests, as had the graying of the population and the concomitant strains an older resident base would place upon the economy.

Stradley and Goodman both touched upon an intangible in their works: Indian gaming. Following the Indian Gaming Regulatory Act's passage in 1988, the state's tribes began to investigate the possibility of building casinos to improve life on their respective reservations. Kathryn R.L. Rand and Steven Andrew Light, both professors at the University of North Dakota, have made careers of studying Indian gaming in the United States. During its 1991 legislative session, the state's governing body created a gaming commission to assume the role rulemaking and enforcement from the Attorney General. In 1992, Governor George Sinner signed compacts allowing North Dakota's five tribes to conduct Class III gaming.[359]

North Dakota is technically home to four Indian Reservations: Turtle Mountain Indian Reservation, Standing Rock Indian Reservation, Spirit Lake Indian Reservation and Fort Berthold Indian Reservation. However, a small portion of the Sisseton-Wahpeton Indian Reservation extends into the southeastern corner of the state. As its headquarters are in South Dakota, the tribe is considered to be resident to that state. However, the presence of Indian lands in North Dakota allow for its entry into the gaming business in the Flickertail State.

Due to their location upon lands not desired by Euro-Americans, many of the tribes of North Dakota live on substandard lands, much of which cannot provide sufficiently for their owners' and families' needs. Indeed, many Native American households live in poverty. At Standing Rock Reservation, the poverty rate in 1990 stood at 59 percent. Frequently homes are without electricity, indoor plumbing, running water or telephones. Unemployment reaches nearly 90 percent on some reservations, resulting in apathy, alcoholism and suicide at rates far above those of their European American neighbors.[360] Hence the possibility of casino gaming struck a central chord among the tribal populations of North Dakota. Herein lay a possible solution to the poverty that gripped the tribes so firmly.

In 1992, the Standing Rock Sioux negotiated the first Indian gaming contract in North Dakota. Other tribes followed in quick succession, providing the state's residents and its visitors Four Bears Lodge and Casino in New Town (Three Affiliated Tribes), Dakotah Magic Casino and Hotel in Hankinson (Sisseton-Wahpeton Sioux), Prairie Knights Casino and Resort at Fort Yates (Standing Rock Sioux), Sky Dancer Hotel and Casino in Belcourt (Turtle Mountain Band of Chippewa) and Spirit Lake Casino and Resort in Spirit Lake (Spirit Lake Sioux). The casinos brought sorely needed money and jobs to the tribal governments and their people, as well as strengthened tribal sovereignty, including but not limited to language preservation and traditional cultural renewal. They also brought social problems in the form of gambling addiction, poor financial decisions and stresses upon family structures unaccustomed to a disposable income.[361]

Prairie Knights Casino, New Town

North Dakota Tourism

Besides drawing local folks, casinos also drew gamblers from out of state, improving tourism, and adding to the state's coffers. Major tourist attractions remained Medora, the International Peace Gardens, the Heritage Center and historic sites, particularly those associated with the Lewis and Clark expedition, the state's native heritage, and its scenic by-ways. Also of importance were recreation tourism, i.e., hunting, fishing, boating, hiking, etc., and, more frequently than in years past, agri-tourism and eco-tourism. Ethnic festivals such as Minot's Höstfest, Native American pow-wows, Fifth of May festivals commemorating Norwegian independence, and agricultural heritage celebrations remained popular.

By the mid 1990s, tourism fell second only to agriculture as North Dakota's primary business, with energy production placing third. Besides the electrical energy produced at the mouth of mines in central North Dakota, as well as the coal gasification plant located near Beulah, another form of energy became increasingly viable and available: wind energy. A study by the Pacific Northwest Laboratory conducted in 1991 suggested that North Dakota had the greatest wind energy potential of any state in the nation. Wind turbines placed in North Dakota, according to the firm, could produce sufficient energy to power 36 percent of the nation's 1990 electrical consumption, or 14,000 times the power usage of the entire state for a year. Although much of the state could be relied upon to produce the winds necessary to move the giant turbine blades in their pathway to energy production, the Missouri and Pembina Escarpments provided the steadiest and strongest winds. By the mid 1990s, the Turtle Mountain Chippewa, as well as the Spirit Lake Sioux had begun the production of wind-driven electrical energy, as had the Richardton Abbey.[362]

Manufacturing came in a strong fourth in terms of importance to the state's economy. Scattered across the state were factories producing Steiger tractors, Case-IH tractors, computer harnesses, business and accounting software, Bobcat skid steers, bricks, pasta, meat products, Kevlar protective coverings for the Department of Defense, frozen processed potatoes and dough, as well as airplanes and airplane parts. Call centers for travel agencies and airline firms also provided employment opportunities for individuals not interested in agricultural production, as did firms producing electrical energy and natural gas.[363]

Given the state's economic position with regard to agricultural prices and production, as well as its declining production of oil, and the proverbial "brain drain" as youth left the state, the electorate had much to consider in selecting candidates for office. The election of 1990 did not provide the excitement of a presidential or gubernatorial contest. Indeed, the only race of significance came in the form of Republican Edward T. Schafer's challenge for North Dakota's sole seat in the United States House of Representatives. Byron Dorgan, Democrat, again stood for the office he had held for the previous nine years. Dorgan won handily, 152,530 to Schafer's 81,443.[364]

In February of 1991, the state legislature undertook a task many felt long overdue; it legalized trade on Sundays, at least in the afternoons. By doing so, it broke with a century-old tradition. Indeed, since its formation as a state, North Dakota law forbade stores to be open on Sundays, as well as public sports, trade, manufacturing, menial labor or the mechanical arts to be practiced. While some scoffed at the "blue" law, others maintained that keeping one day a week sacred from labors and commercial distractions kept North Dakotans morally fit and familially strong.[365]

While the majority of pulpits supported Sunday closures in the name of maintaining strong families, merchants, particularly those living in towns bordering Minnesota, South Dakota and Montana, perceived only lost revenue. Despite several years of attempts, however, the legislature remained firm in its belief that the Sabbath should be maintained, even if a few baseball games did get played, and a few movies viewed. Facing financial arguments that seemed irrefutable, however, the legislature turned its back on one hundred years of tradition and began allowing businesses to open at noon on Sundays. A few businesses, such as restaurants, funeral homes, tourist attractions, power and fuel generation and distribution, as well as libraries, could open before 12:00 p.m., the rest were to remain shuttered until the afternoon.[366]

Taxable sales for the first quarter of 1992 rose by nine percent over the same period of 1991. Despite the rising in retail sales, many still opposed the change, feeling that all laborers deserved at least one day of rest. Particularly disturbed were the owners of small family-owned businesses that now felt obligated to open on Sunday in competition to chain stores, meaning, of course, that at least one family member was absent from family affairs, tending to business.[367]

Another great change to North Dakota in 1992 came with the September 8, death of long-term Democratic Congressman Quentin N. Burdick. Having served slightly over twenty-eight years in the Senate and, along the way, having achieved considerable stature within the Senate due to his seniority, Burdick's death threatened to reduce the power of the North Dakota delegation in the United States Congress. The stakes for finding the appropriate replacement seemed rather high. Governor Sinner graciously appointed Burdick's widow Jocelyn Birch Burdick to fill his unexpired term until a special election could be called. Given the short time between Burdick's death and the forthcoming general election, Sinner determined to hold a special election to fill the senator's seat on December 4, 1992.[368]

Mildly put, the race proved interesting. In the spring of 1992, Senator Kent Conrad announced that he would not seek re-election in the autumn. At his initial election in 1986, he pledged not to stand for re-election should the federal budget deficit not fall by the 1992 election. Although undoubtedly popular enough to win the post for a second term, he remained constant to his vow. However, with the death of Senator Burdick, Conrad changed his mind and determined to stand for election. In the meantime, Democratic Representative Byron Dorgan was elected to fill the post vacated by Conrad. In the November 3, 1992, election he handily defeated Republican Steve Sydness, 179,347 to 118,162. Earl Pomeroy, Democrat and former state insurance commissioner, easily won the state's lone seat in the United States House of Representatives by defeating Republican John T. Korsmo, 169,273 to 117,442.[369]

Also at state-level politics, Republican Edward T. Schafer defeated Democratic candidate Nicholas Spaeth, 176,398 to 123,845. Schafer's running mate Rosemarie Myrdal was only the second woman in North Dakota history to hold the position of lieutenant governor.[370]

Congressman Earl Pomeroy

Courtesy, Representative Earl Pomeroy's Office.

Governor Edward T. Schafer

Courtesy of Edward T. Schafer, North Dakota Governor, 1992–2000, U. S. Secretary of Agriculture, 2008

With regard to the election for president of the United States, no surprise occurred. As they traditionally do, North Dakotans cast their ballots for the Republican, incumbent George H.W. Bush, offering him 136,244 votes to the 99,168 gained by the eventual winner Bill Clinton.[371]

In the special election to fill the recently deceased Quentin Burdick's seat, held December 4, 1992, Senator Kent Conrad, Democrat, canvassed 103,246 to Jack Dalrymple's 55,194. Then came the confusion. Once Conrad won the remaining years of Burdick's term, he resigned the senate seat he held as a result of his 1986 election. Accordingly, Conrad maintained his seniority in the Senate, having served continuously, albeit as a victor in two widely dispersed elections. Governor Sinner then appointed the newly elected Byron Dorgan to fill the remaining month of Conrad's first term. By doing so, Dorgan gained a competitive advantage in the Senate with regard to committee appointments, office space, etc. The House seat just won by Earl Pomeroy had to remain temporarily vacant; the United States Constitution prohibits a House member from serving by appointment.[372]

The election of 1994 offered no such confusing excitement. Kent Conrad, standing for re-election on the remaining years of Burdick's term claimed the votes of 137,157 North Dakotans, while Dr. Ben Clayburgh, Republican, gained only 99,390. Earl Pomeroy returned to the House by a 17,000 vote margin over Republican Gary Porter and Independent James Germalic.[373]

The problems faced by North Dakotans in the early 1990s could not be declared to be new ones. Rather they were intensifications of issues identified in earlier decades. Farmers continued to suffer from problems with prices and precipitation, youth still sought adventure and economic gain outside the confines of North Dakota, manufacturers struggled to claim a share of the market, the population still fluttered between growth and loss, and political power continued to sway between Democrats and Republicans.

chapter 9

THE MILLENNIUM ENDS
The Latter 1990s

For many residents of North Dakota, the decade from 1985 through 1994 could only be considered a difficult one. The farm and energy crisis struck at the state's economic core, drought gripped the region, elitist Easterners proposed seemingly ludicrous theories about deprivatizing the land, and population numbers continued to trend downward. The census of 1990 revealed a North Dakota population of 638,800, a statistically significant drop of two percent from the 652,717 residents recorded in 1980. Moreover, during the first years of the century's last decade, the state's population continued to drop. Demographers estimated in 1991, for example, that the population of North Dakota stood at 634,199.[374]

By the mid 1990s, however, it appeared that the worst was over, and that the state's population would commence to trend upward. Indeed, there was some indication that the farm and energy crises had drawn to their conclusion, and that new residents, by birth or immigration, could be counted on to recoup some of the state's lost population. By 1996, the demographers estimated North Dakota's population at 642,858. The jubilation, however, was short-lived: by the decade's close, the population of North Dakota fell to approximately 633,666 residents.[375]

As in previous years, the greatest population declines took place in the western portions of the state, with the few counties gaining population already centers of business, education or government. For example, of the fourteen counties located in the geographical slope west of the Missouri River, only one gained population: Morton. Undoubtedly Morton County's success came from the fact that it lay immediately next to Bismarck and the employment offered by state government. Burleigh County, actual site of the state capitol, also rose in population. Only six counties of fifty-three gained population from 1990 to 1999.[376]

Other counties gaining population might easily have been predicted. Sioux and Rolette counties, with their relatively youthful residents, gained population. Indeed, an examination of median ages in the state revealed that these two counties had the youngest average age of population of any counties in the state. Sioux County's median age stood at 22.9 years of age in 1990 and 23.9 in 2000. For Rolette County, comparative figures were 26.6 and 28.9. Of course, it is the comparatively young adults who produce the next generation of children, as opposed to the residents of McIntosh County, whose median ages 48.5 (1990) and 51.0 (2000) did not portend well for further reproduction.[377]

In addition, Ward County, home to Minot and Minot State University gained population, as did Cass County. Indeed, over the decade, Cass County gained nearly 16,000 residents, more than the population of many western counties combined. With education, government, industry, transportation, business, entertainment and general service opportunities available, little wonder could be found in the flocking to Fargo and its environs. Grand Forks County, home of the state's largest educational institution, as well as its largest air force base, actually lost population over the course of the decade. The severe flooding of 1997 undoubtedly contributed to the loss of residents.[378]

While it is clear that many of the new residents of Cass County came from the hinterlands of North Dakota, another factor must also be taken into consideration. Between 1993 and 2000, over three thousand individuals immigrated to North Dakota from foreign lands. The majority of these migrants ended up living in urban areas where social support services and kindred souls could be accessed with relative ease. Besides Canada, the legal immigrants came in the largest numbers from the former Soviet Union, Vietnam and India. Estimates of illegal immigrants ranged as high as six thousand individuals. People came to North Dakota from over thirty different nations.[379]

Essentially matching the number of legal immigrants to North Dakota over the course of the 1990s came the loss in the number of farms. From 1990 to 1999, the state lost 2,500 farms, and presumptively as many farmers and their families from the land. As the number of farmers declined, the acreage for which each was responsible rose. In 1990, the average-sized farm/ranch operation stood at 1,209 acres. By 1999, the average size had risen to nearly 1,300 acres.[380]

Farmland prices continued to rise over the closing years of the decade. Land in the northern end of the Red River Valley which had sold for about $640/acre in 1990, brought approximately $800/acre in the latter 1990s, with Pembina County land selling for slightly over $1,000/acre, a state record. In the southern end of the valley, land fetched approximately $850/acre, up from $750/acre a half decade before. In the central portion of the state, land in the northern half could be expected to sell for about $350/acre, while that in the southern half for approximately $300/acre. And, as always, land in the slope, generally used for grazing, sold for the least per acre. Most land beyond the Missouri River could be purchased for about $250/acre.[381]

As the price of land rose, the implication prevailed that conditions for the state's farmers and ranchers was improving. However, little could be further from the truth. Roger Johnson, North Dakota Commissioner of Agriculture, painted a rather grim picture in testimony before the United States House of Representatives Agricultural Committee. In testimony presented in June 2000, Johnson reflected on the conditions of his home state's agriculturalists. According to his statistics, both wheat and cattle produced only nominal returns for their producers; indeed, wheat from 1997-99, actually returned less than its cost of production. Cattle returned less than their cost of production in 1995 and 1996, and less than $25 per animal profit in 1997 and 1998. The comparatively low prices had been exacerbated by bad weather, severe flooding and crop diseases according to Johnson.[382]

Roger Johnson, Commissioner of Agriculture

Courtesy, North Dakota Department of Agriculture

Registered Black Angus, St. Anthony

Ellingson Angus Ranch, St. Anthony, N.D. Photo Courtesy of the Beef CheckOff-funded web site, www.BeefFromPastureToPlate.org.

The continually rising cost of inputs contributed to the relatively low profit margin. Before a farmer could consider the year to be a success, with regard to grain production, he needed to subtract the expenses associated with planting, growing and harvesting: seed, fertilizer, pesticides, fuel, repairs and hired labor. With livestock, the rancher needed to consider feed, veterinary supplies and services, as well as feeder livestock. Such expenses had essential doubled over the previous ten years.[303]

Probably the most significant element for most farmers came in the form of fuel. As Johnson observed, "Full gas tanks aren't an expendable option on farming operations—it takes fuel to plant, cultivate, fertilize, harvest and transport crops from farmers to market." Congress, he suggested, should "closely investigate the extraordinary increases in gasoline and fuel prices." Moreover, pesticide costs had tripled over the previous decade, according to Johnson. Strangely, United States farmers paid approximately 40 percent more for their pesticides than their Canadian competitors for virtually identical products. Congress needed to act before the limited profitability remaining in agriculture was squeezed out.[384]

With skyrocketing prices for agricultural inputs—chemical expenses per farming operation stood at approximately $14,000 in 1999, while total expenses associated with planting a crop or raising cattle averaged $160,000 per operation—the need for greater return on agricultural production became paramount. This, however, was not to be. Corn, which had returned $2.28/bushel in 1990 fell to a $1.82/bushel by 1999. Flax started the decade at $5.27/bushel and concluded it at $3.79/bushel, while soybeans fell from $5.74/bushel in 1990 to $4.63/bushel in 1999. Sunflower prices also dipped during the decade, falling from $10.80/cwt. to $7.53/cwt.[385]

Undifferentiated wheat, North Dakota's number one agricultural product also fell significantly in price during the 1990s. From $2.61/bushel in 1990, it rose in value to $4.55/bushel in 1995. However, by 1999, the price declined to a decade low of $2.48/bushel. North Dakota is the nation's single largest producer of durum wheat. That, however, does not provide a monopoly or allow North Dakota farmers to set their own prices based upon the expenses incurred in production. In 1995, durum sold for $5.65/bushel, but it fell to $2.73/bushel by 1999. Sugar beets fell by approximately $8/ton from 1996 to 1999. Beef ranchers did not have the best of worlds in the latter 1990s either. In 1993, fat steers sold for $75.82/cwt. By 1998 the price had fallen to $61.43/cwt.[386]

As always, some farmers and ranchers attempted to find new ways to make a profit from their land. While some turned their attention to organic farming, others tried to raise buffalo, touting it as a leaner red meat than beef. Still others turned to value-added agriculture, producing specialized pastas and sauces, soups, honeys, and exotic vegetables. Others turned to fee hunting, as discussed earlier, as well as to providing eco-tourism experiences to urbanites on working ranches. Some have turned to leading birding groups and nature hikes in an effort to save the family farm.[387]

Beyond economizing and attempting new ventures, more and more farm wives found themselves on the job market. Quite frequently a wife's "town job", as opposed to her work on the farm, would demarcate success or failure for the family's agricultural operation. Not only did paid employment off the farm provide an infusion of cash into the family economy every two weeks, it also often provided much-needed health insurance benefits. Health benefits often out-weighed the significance of the minimal pay most women received in their small-town employment. Also taking to town work to support the family's farming or ranching operation were husbands and fathers, albeit in lesser numbers than wives and mothers. After working a full day, perhaps for an implement dealer, a fertilizer dealer, or a manufacturing plant, or even for a more successful neighboring farmer, the man of the family would return to his own farming operation to work into the night. Older children, teenagers for the most part, often contributed their labor to the farm or ranch, as well as held part time jobs to contribute to the family's income, as well as attending high school.[388]

As some farms and ranches failed, the communities nearby underwent significant change. For example, during the latter 1990s, many churches found themselves unable to pay a pastor, lacking sufficient congregants to meet the expense. For some this meant closure, for others alternate solutions. In the case of Griggs, Eddy and Foster counties, the solution came in the form of Tri-County Ministries. Eight struggling churches (seven Lutheran and one Presbyterian) joined together to support four pastors, each of whom was responsible for providing two sermons each Sunday, but who also rotated among the churches. Not only did the system provide pastors for rural congregations, but it also provided a sense of community for rural ministers who often felt isolated in their missions.[389]

Educators also felt the strain of changing North Dakota demographics. As the median age for the state's residents rose, as young men and women and their reproductive capacities left the rural areas of North Dakota or the state all together, and as parents had fewer children than in generations previous, the number of children available for schooling in North Dakota dropped considerably. Indeed, statistics illustrate quite easily the declining number of births within the state. In 1982, 12,655 children were born in North Dakota, in 1996, 8,336 babies came into the world here, a 34 percent decline. Although not felt immediately—children do not generally start school until age 5—the impact on the public education system of the state would prove dramatic. In 1994-95, 118,649 students attended classes in the state's public schools. In 2006-07, the number had declined by 19 percent to 95,600 students. The future, according to Tom Decker, Director of Finance, Department of Public Instruction, did not look bright. By 2017-18, the estimated enrollment in the public schools of North Dakota would be 85,530 pupils, a decline on an additional 11 percent.[390]

Historically speaking, the number of school districts in North Dakota dropped continuously since the late 1910s. In 1918, for example, there were 4,700 independent school districts. Granted, the majority of these districts represented one-room schools, but still a rural population needed this level of educational access. By 1947, following reorganization policies formulated on the state level, the number of school districts dropped to slightly over 2,200. By 1961, this number had been halved, leaving the state with 1,021 districts and reflecting changing educational needs and population trends. Yet, further cuts in the number of school districts awaited. In 1973, only 364 districts existed in the state, and in 1992, that number had again fallen, this time to 270 districts. And by 2000, following years of agricultural distress, as well as declining birthrates and an aging population, North Dakota had just 230 school districts.[391]

Illustrating a trend towards urbanization, Department of Public Instruction figures revealed that more students attended Fargo, West Fargo, Grand Forks, Minot, Bismarck, Mandan, Dickinson and Jamestown schools than the rest of the state combined. As parents seek the best education possible for their children, it is entirely feasible that the largest districts will grow even more to the detriment of the smaller school districts. Small districts often cannot offer the variety of courses or the depth of instruction available in the larger school districts. Where one teacher in a small district may be expected to cover history, geography, economics and government, in a larger district there may be several teachers devoted to any one single topic.[392]

As the number of high school graduates in the state falls, North Dakota's universities and colleges will ultimately feel the stress. Schools must recruit more actively from outside the state and nation, lower admission standards or witness declines in enrollment. The question arises as to who will fill the positions requiring advanced education. Young professionals trained elsewhere are not necessarily eager to start their careers in a region that they are unfamiliar with, and which traditionally offers lower starting salaries than other regions of the nation. Many young North Dakotans feel an initial wanderlust following their collegiate education, and often forego North Dakota employment opportunities.[393]

The entirety of the situation leaves North Dakota in a precarious situation with regard to its population: an aging population needs resources, a widely dispersed population needs significant infrastructure, the state's young professionals must be financially rewarded to remain in the state (particularly after the state has assumed considerable expense in their post-secondary education), manufacturing requires tax incentives, as do service industries, and resources are, of course, finite.

Farming remains the largest single segment of the North Dakota economy. While manufacturing once held second place, it has in recent years been replaced by tourism as a major revenue stream. In 1999, tourism brought $2.6 billion into the state, or 28 percent of the state's revenue. This marked an increase of more than 500 percent since 1990. Although the state itself spent approximately $2.2 million per year on tourism promotion, it still ranked a dismal 50th in terms of state expenditures on promoting attractions. And, despite the funds expended, in a query of over 10,000 individual from outside the state, North Dakota came in 47th as a desired destination. That said, most certainly people were visiting North Dakota, absorbing its cultural, historical, natural and tourist-oriented attractions. As the 20th century drew to a close, excitement about the forthcoming bicentennial of the Lewis and Clark Expedition brought thousands to North Dakota. Also attracting significant interest were vacations centered on activities: hiking, birding, hunting, fishing, dinosaur-fossil digs, horseback riding, and water-oriented sports such as sailing, boating, swimming, etc.[394]

Indian gaming or casinos attracted considerable attention both from North Dakotans and from visitors over the latter portion of the 1990s. With five casinos scattered across the state to select from, interested parties could find not only gambling opportunities, but also often hotel accommodations and frequently yesterday's headliner entertainment.[395]

For those seeking a more traditional tourist-oriented vacation, Medora provided faux-western-facades, restored historic buildings, and access to the Badlands, as well as bumper cars, golf courses, fancy coffee, and modern hotels. The Medora Musical, a harmonized and fictionalized account of the town's historic past, including Theodore Roosevelt and the Marquis de Mores, drew over 110,000 visitors each year as the 1990s came to a close.[396]

Bully Pulpit Golf Course, Medora
North Dakota Tourism/Wade Westin

Manufacturing came in third in terms of a contribution to the state's economy throughout the late 1990s. Due to its somewhat isolated status, North Dakota's economic development agencies did not, and do not, attract significant large-scale manufacturers to the state. The region's distance from many significant raw materials, as well as the expense of hauling such materials into a manufacturing plant, make it difficult to sell the region to businesses contemplating moving or starting operations. However, businesses currently located in North Dakota, or entrepreneurs seeking opportunities, were, and are, much more likely to open new concerns or expand existing ones. North Dakota's laborers have a reputation of working hard and providing a full day's labor for a full day's pay.

Throughout the latter part of the 1990s, North Dakotans made such widely disparate items as bricks, skid steers, pasta, frozen potato products, frozen dough products, sugar, computer software, computer harnesses, electrical energy, natural gas, Case IH tractors, packed beef, fabricated metal products, airplanes, cabinetry and wind turbines, among a host of other products. Approximately 23,000 North Dakotans made their living in some aspect of manufacturing. Wages received by these laborers fell somewhat below the national average for manufacturing employees.[397]

In addition, many North Dakotans made their livings in service industries. Call centers for hotel and airline reservations offered some individuals employment, while others worked in health care, information services, education, state and federal government, the United States Air Force, the United States Border Patrol, law enforcement, etc. Of course, small enterprises involved in the production of services abounded, including Indian gaming.

Indian gaming brings a considerable financial impact to the state of North Dakota. With regard to Spirit Lake Casino and Resort, one scholar has estimated the employment of approximately 400 Native Americans, frequently drawn straight from the welfare roles of the state. Eighty percent of the employees at Spirit Lake Casino are from the Spirit Lake Sioux Nation. However, not only Native Americans benefit from the presence of casinos in North Dakota. Supplies to operate the casinos, including such things as soap, food, uniforms, electrical service, furniture and the like are generally purchased in the community, hence providing a profitable arrangement for non-tribal individuals. A 2000 estimate suggests that the gaming industry employs nearly 2,000 individuals with a payroll of c. $30 million per year in the state. The multiplier effect of this payroll results in a $121.7 million economic benefit to North Dakota. Beyond the direct and indirect financial impact, the result for the state's reservations has been substantial. Not only has a sense of pride been restored to men and women with gainful employment, but also funds generated by the casinos have gone to upgrade the infrastructure of the reservations. Many of the reservations now have better health care, educational facilities, recreational opportunities and small business loan availability than ever before.[398]

The energy industry remained a significant portion of North Dakota's economy during the latter 1990s, yet not at the level to which it rose in the latter 1980s. North Dakota ranked 9th among oil-producing states in terms of production, providing approximately two percent of the oil extracted in the United States. Not only did oil benefit the state in terms of its sheer production, sales, employment and refinement, it also provided revenue in the form of an extraction tax and a production tax. Throughout the closing years of the decade, the taxes produced approximately $30 million in revenue per annum.[399]

In general, every barrel of crude oil pumped from the western lands of North Dakota brings with it 800 cubic feet of natural gas. Coupled with "natural" natural gas, North Dakota is one of only two states to produce synthetic natural gas, and has the largest synthetic production plant in the nation. The Great Plains Synfuels Plant in Beulah annually produces 54 billion cubic feet of gas from lignite. In total, North Dakota produces approximately one percent of the nation's natural gas supply.[400]

Lignite mining and processing remained an essential part of the 1990s North Dakota economy. Nearly all of the coal mined in the state remained in the state, however, predominantly to produce electrical energy, the majority of which was exported to Midwestern states. To facilitate the inexpensive production of electricity, power plants were often located at the mouth of the mine in order to save transportation costs on the lignite. Typically in a modern surface-mining operation, the overburden of soil was removed using dragline buckets capable of moving 30 cubic yards of dirt or more. The lignite was then blasted from place and loaded with power shovels into enormous trucks for delivery to the power plant. In the latter 1990s, approximately 3,700 men and women worked directly to make this process possible. Another 15,000 indirectly labored to supply the needs of those mining the lignite. All told, lignite generated more than $1.2 billion in business activity, and added more than $60 million in tax revenues to the state's coffers.[401]

Strip mine, Falkirk Mine, near Underwood

Airphoto - Jim Wark

Promising to provide a renewable energy source, wind turbines came more and more into use during the closing days of the century. For example, at Sacred Heart Monastery in Richardton, Benedictine sisters began generating nearly 50 percent of their own electrical energy from two wind turbines installed in 1997. The towers stand 80 feet tall with turbine blades of nearly 23 feet. Although not of the latest vintage, the turbines have proven their worth to the sisters of Sacred Heart. Moreover, that North Dakota maintains an average wind speed of approximately 14 to 15 miles per hour or greater, means that the state provides potential to lessen residents', and Americans in general, reliance on non-renewable energy sources. Based upon this fact, LM Glasfiber, the largest wind turbine blade manufacturer in the world began producing turbine blades in Grand Forks in 1999, employing 75 individuals.[402]

Wind was but one phenomenon of nature to be contended with in the latter 1990s. At times, Mother Nature gave the distinct impression that she might be angry with the state, particularly in 1996 and 1997. As officially recognized by the National Weather Service, the winter of 1996-97 pounded the state with nine blizzards, starting in November and lasting into April. Many regions of the state set records for their annual snowfall totals as a result of that peculiar winter. Bismarck, for example, had 102 inches of snow, and Fargo 117 inches for records. Not record setting, but still thoroughly disturbing, Grand Forks had 98 inches and Jamestown 103 inches of the white stuff. Many times the accompanying winds forced wind chill conditions of 60 degrees below zero, or more. Indeed, in early January 1997, wind chills of 80 degrees below zero wracked the state. Conditions were so bad that on January 12, 1997, President Bill Clinton issued a disaster declaration for the entirety of the state, ordering federal aid to assist the state with snow removal efforts. It would not be the only disaster declaration of the season.[403]

As the snow melted upstream, flooding occurred in a number of locations: Mott, Beulah, Wahpeton, Fargo, etc. However, the Red River of the North unleashed its greatest fury against the community of Grand Forks. All throughout the last days of March and through mid-April 1997, residents knew the threat for flooding was considerable. Accordingly, they filled and placed hundreds of thousands of sandbags, built clay dikes along the eastern side of the town, and then topped them with sandbags and even boards. Regardless of the efforts undertaken, the Red kept rising, rising and rising some more. The National Weather Service's initial predictions kept rising, rising and rising yet again. Finally, it appeared that the residents of Grand Forks might win their battle. Protection against the predicted 48-foot crest seemed feasible. Just one year before, residents had protected the city to 45.8 feet.[404]

The Red, however, rose to 54.11 feet, and all of the efforts of the thousands of volunteers fell to naught. At first water spilled into the Lincoln Drive neighborhood, but soon overspread the city, both by simply flooding and also by storm sewer transfer. By Saturday, April 19, four feet of water flowed through the streets and buildings of downtown Grand Forks. In other areas only a foot or two covered the streets, but in the low-lying regions of Lincoln and Riverside Parks water covered houses to their second story. Lacking potable water, safe residences, electricity, sewer service and a modern city's infrastructure, the vast majority of Grand Forks and East Grand Forks, Minnesota's, residents evacuated their homes. University of North Dakota President Kendall Baker closed the campus a mere two weeks before the end of the semester, easing the burden on the city's protective services and offering some semblance of safety to the 11,500 students enrolled there.[405]

As citizens fled their homes and their city, in their rear view mirrors, they beheld the most amazing of scenes. Not only had their city flooded, now it burned. At 4:15 p.m. a fire alarm sounded in the Security Building in the downtown. Most probably started by an electrical short, the fire presented innumerable problems. Most significantly, there did not seem to be a way by which the fire department could draw close enough to the fire to actually attack it. Only after the passage of several hours did the Grand Forks Fire Department rig fire trucks on the back of low-boy trailers enabling their engines to function and effectively draft water from the river that swirled around them. Planes dropped fire retardant on the flames, while helicopters filled leather buckets with water from the river to drop upon the flames. In slightly over twelve hours, eleven historic buildings had either been destroyed or significantly damaged. The irony was lost on very few.[406]

In the midst of it all, President Bill Clinton visited the cities, promising a minimum of $500 million in flood relief. Reflecting on the communities' spirit he noted "water cannot wash that away, fire cannot burn that away, and a blizzard cannot freeze that away." Other relief came from "the Angel", later identified as McDonald's heiress Joan Kroc, who issued checks of up to $2,000 per affected household. Individuals came from across the nation, and Canada, to help Grand Forks residents clean up and commence the rebuilding of their lives. Also coming from across the nation were donations of goods, money, food and clothing. Charitable organizations created their own flood, arriving in town with cleaning kits, hot meals, physical assistance, moral support and divine guidance.[407]

While the floods made life miserable for urban dwellers, life was also made difficult for farmers and ranchers over the long winter of 1996-97. Throughout the multiple blizzards which struck North Dakota that winter, ranchers could not always tend to their livestock. Officials estimated that at least 125,000 head of cattle died that winter. During the floods, thousands of cattle perished from starvation, disease and drowning. For other farmers the problem came with fields that simply would not dry out in time for planting in 1996 or 1997, or which were littered with the debris of flotsam carried by the waters of the Red and other rivers. The excessive moisture also promoted plant diseases.[408]

Flooding did not just occur along the rivers and streams of North Dakota in the springtime due to snow melt. As the result of a prolonged wet cycle, Devils Lake, commencing in 1993, began to rise. Within seven years, the lake rose slightly more than 25 feet. In the process, a lake that stood at 40,000 acres for generations grew to 122,000 acres, absorbing 75,000 acres of farmland. Not only farmland fell under the rising lake. As it spread, Devils Lake claimed 300 homes and at least 100 buildings. Most were moved to higher ground; however, some were abandoned in place. The federal government purchased the entire community of Churchs Ferry, on the northwest side of the lake, for $3.5 million, relocating 109 individuals in the process. Roads and bridges which once easily carried traffic above the water level were replaced, and then replaced again. In 2000, $35 million was spent on road re-building alone.[409]

For some, the natural solution to the continuously rising lake was an outlet to the Sheyenne River which would ultimately drain Devils Lake into the Red River and northward to Canada; however, not all saw that solution as feasible, or legal. Canadians voiced their concerns about the possibility of non-native fish species and parasites, as well as other biota, contaminating provincial waters. Sulfate levels also caused concern among some Canadians. So while North Dakotans sought a solution in an outlet, Manitobans dragged their feet, calling upon the 1909 Boundary Waters Treaty Act as a preventive measure. In 1999, the United States Army Corps of Engineers withdrew from the plan to build an outlet. North Dakotans determined to move ahead on their own terms.[410]

Among those supportive of measures to reduce the level of Devils Lake via an outlet to the Sheyenne River was North Dakota Governor Edward T. Schafer. Elected in 1992, Schafer, in his initial term, faced the farm crisis, the oil field crisis, the rising waters of Devils Lake, and what he perceived as a rather negative national image of North Dakota. The state's voters apparently agreed that he had faced these difficulties with strength and forethought. Accordingly, he easily won re-election in 1996, defeating the Democratic challenger Lee Kaldor by approximately 85,000 votes. Also retaining his seat was United States Representative Earl Pomeroy, although by not quite so handy a margin, over Kevin Cramer.[411]

On the national level, as with tradition, North Dakotans cast the majority of their ballots for the Republican candidate for president, Bob Dole. Dole gained the votes of 125,050 citizens, with his Democratic competitor Bill Clinton gathering the votes of 106,905. Clinton, of course, handily won the national election, claiming his second term of office.[412]

The interim election of 1998 drew considerable attention, albeit for a Senate Resolution's presence on the ballot. The resolution called for the removal of references to the names, locations and missions of the state's institutions of higher education from the constitution. While members of the legislature claimed that separating names, responsibilities and locations of institutions in the constitution would make for greater flexibility in governance, not all saw the measure so benignly. Smaller communities, often home to institutions of higher learning, as well as their neighboring communities, perceived that separating the elements would allow for the easier closure of the smaller colleges. With the proposed amendment in place, a simple vote of the legislature could alter the face of higher education in North Dakota. Otherwise, a constitutional amendment would be required to alter each institution's mission. The measure was soundly defeated by North Dakota voters, 123,278 to 70,403.[413]

In the same election, Byron Dorgan easily won re-election to the United States Senate, and Earl Pomeroy did likewise to the United States House of Representatives, respectively defeating Republicans Donna Nalawaja and Kevin Cramer.[414]

As the century, as well as the millennium, came to a close, North Dakotans faced a number of critical questions and challenges. The "brain drain" of youth out migration, the troubled agricultural economy, the aging population, the difficulty in attracting quality manufacturing concerns, the generally low standard of living and the power of the natural environment would, among other issues, provide for more than one sleepless night for the men and women who led the state into the next century.

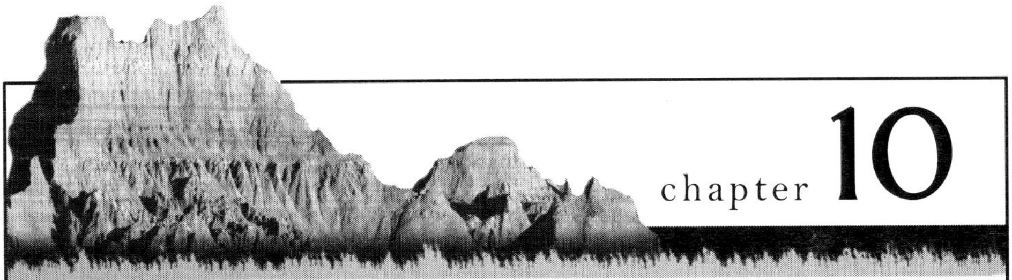

chapter 10

EPILOGUE: WHAT MIGHT THE FUTURE HOLD?

The New Millennium

By no means is history a predictive science. For those who want some sense of sure footing, let them turn to those social sciences or hard sciences with theories, rules and defined parameters of study. Still, studying history in depth, looking for its patterns, allows for some consideration of the future as rooted in the past. With that in mind, a few suggestions as to the future of North Dakota might be in order, if only to be referred to in the future as another historian gone wrong.

Since the 1920s, the youth of North Dakota have sought to leave the farm. At first they took refuge in the state's urban centers: Grand Forks, Fargo, Bismarck, Minot and the like. However, as the knowledge of new opportunities spread, particularly after the Second World War and technology made for easier moves, more and more young men and women left the state in pursuit of their economic, cultural and personal goals. While it may be personally painful to see our children leave the state, a larger public problem looms: maintaining a significant population. The state needs and will continue to need bright energetic individuals to pursue all realms of economic development: agriculture, manufacturing, service industries, government, etc. Without the presence of the young men and young women that the state has invested in via education and social services, the state's economy will stagnate. Young adults add vitality to a community and bring with them new perspectives and new ideas. They are our human capital.

Young men and young women are the parents of the following generation. Without the presence of these parents, grandparents will be visiting their grandchildren in cities and states far from their North Dakota homes. Accordingly, fewer schools, fewer churches, fewer restaurants and fewer clinics, among other services, will be needed in the future. School consolidations and school closings will be a continuing discussion for the foreseeable future. A state with a median age of 38.8 years of age cannot easily reproduce itself.[4.15]

Concomitant with a youthful population on the move is an aging population base. Individuals are living longer than ever before. And while some of the elderly, for statistical purposes those over the age of 65, may leave the state for warmer climates and continued contact with children and grandchildren, North Dakotans have a tendency to age in place. The majority does not move from their primary residence or community until ill health makes remaining in place an impossibility. Moreover, North Dakotans often return home to family and friends following careers outside the state, elevating the average age of population. At the census of 2000, nearly 15 percent of North Dakotans were over 65 years of age. For many counties, particularly the more rural and western ones, the number of elderly far exceeds 15 percent. Additionally, North Dakota has the highest proportion of any state of individuals over the age of 85. If current trends run true, 23 percent of the state's population will be over 65 years of age in 2020.[+16] The discerning question remains: "How do we best attend to the needs of an elderly population, particularly in the absence of a youthful one?"

With study, other trends in population become apparent. Perhaps the most obvious of these is the movement from rural to urban locations. While some of this is reflected in the movement of youth to the eastern portion of the state for educational purposes, their parents are also on the move. As farming becomes less and less profitable due to the rising costs of inputs such as labor, fuel, pesticides, fertilizers, seed, feed and feeder livestock, fewer and fewer farmers and ranchers can maintain their operations. Although federal subsidies have been beneficial, they cannot make up for a series of drought years, blizzard years, or years so wet that crops cannot be planted. Young men and women are eschewing agricultural careers for the stability of a steady paycheck. Those that would like to enter farming or ranching find the initial expenses so exorbitant that they cannot begin an operation. By the start of the millennium, birth or marriage seemed to be the only mechanism by which to enter farming or ranching. The average age of North Dakota's farmers currently stands at 54.4 years.[+17] With little doubt, the size of farms/ranches in North Dakota will continue to expand, while the number of individuals engaged in agricultural pursuits lessens, as well as ages. What will become of North Dakota's single most important economic element if such trends continue?

When he assumed office, Governor Edward T. Schafer made one of his goals the expansion and diversification of manufacturing interests in the state. This has been difficult and will continue to remain problematic. North Dakota is distant from the majority of raw materials essential to manufacturing operations: iron ore, copper, a large population base, etc. It is generally less expensive to haul the raw products produced in North Dakota to distant destinations rather than to construct manufacturing plants in the state and to haul limited raw materials to them. Moreover, most new factories are built in areas where the weather does not require structures to withstand gale force winds and dozens of inches of snow each winter, as well as in locations that do not require the facilities to be heated the majority of the year.

Manufacturing, more appropriately processing, as it does diversify in the state will undoubtedly play upon the region's plentiful agricultural produce. The state is already home to pasta plants, beef and bison processing firms, frozen dough and potato facilities, as well as sugar refineries and flaxseed and flour mills. Of course, its coal deposits are generally transformed to electrical energy in place and a portion of its oil is refined here as well. Without doubt, these sectors of the economy will remain profitable and most probably expand, as will the service industries associated with call centers for hotel and airline reservations, and sales.

Tourism has considerable potential for growth, particularly in light of poor exchange rates for the American dollar abroad. As domestic vacations become more fashionable and financially rational, it is expected that more and more families and individuals will discover the scenic, historic and cultural opportunities available in the state. Travel associated with hunting and fishing will most probably remain profitable for the limited number of outfitters operating in the state, although the potential for over supply is always present. Eco-tourism and agri-tourism should grow in popularity over the next generation or two.

Federal dollars have been important to North Dakota since its beginning. Federal monies supported military encampments, railroad construction and annuity payments to its native peoples. This remains true today, and will continue to be so into the foreseeable future. At present, to name but a few, federal dollars support agricultural subsidies, airport construction and maintenance, Grand Forks and Minot Air Force Bases, highway construction and maintenance, the United States Border Patrol, significant grants to the state's educational institutions, including the Energy and Environmental Research Center and the United States Department of Agriculture Human Nutrition Laboratory. From 1986 to 2003, federal dollars flowing into North Dakota rose from $2,793,135,000 to $5,725,674 per year. In 2005, North Dakota received $1.39 in return for every $1.00 its citizenry paid in federal income taxes. In comparison, the national average was $.91 and Minnesota's average was $.19. Undoubtedly with one of the most senior congressional teams in the nation in Washington, D.C., the funds will keep flowing.[418]

Considerable federal tax monies are returned to North Dakota in response to its natural environment. Flooding along the Red River of the North and its tributaries, blizzards requiring the National Guard's assistance to clear roads, locate stranded motorists and drop hay to isolated herds of cattle, and drought conditions so severe as to require federal intervention for agricultural subsidies, all bring funds into the state. Such natural elements will, as well, continue to wreak havoc with the state's population and reputation.

In his autobiography, *Not So Wild a Dream*, native son Eric Sevareid declared:

> *Why have I not returned for so many years? Why have so few from those prairies ever returned? Where is its written chapter in the long and varied American story? In distant cities when someone would ask: "Where are you from?" and I would answer: "North Dakota," they would merely nod politely and change the subject, having no point of common reference. They knew no one else from there. It was a large, rectangular blank spot in the nation's mind.*[419]

In the present, the state does not remain so much a "blank spot" as it is a place where natural disasters occur and a hearty, if somewhat reticent, people live. North Dakotans, and those who love the state from afar, endure not only deprecating comments from their own, but also from considerable distances. The catalog of slights encountered include the 1989 edition of the Rand-McNally atlas that omitted the entire state, a 1995 article appearing in the *New York Times Magazine* questioning "Is the State of North Dakota

Necessary?', and that *TV Nation's* Michael Moore once sent a film crew to discover why North Dakota was the least visited state in the nation. Unfortunately, they arrived during a blizzard, allowing them to film a nearly abandoned Hector Airport in Fargo.[420] Clearly North Dakotans have an image problem that must be directly dealt with if the state is to prosper. Snow, cold, ethnic jokes, Lawrence Welk and desolation must give way in the nation's mindset to images of healthy, vibrant and intelligent inhabitants, the pleasures of four seasons, a diversifying economy, as well as a diversifying population.

The decisions North Dakotans face in the coming decades are substantial; they are hard. However, on an outside brick bank wall in Sheyenne, a motto peals, but also stands as advice for those who fear for the state's future: "Nothing was ever lost by an enduring faith in North Dakota."

Suggestions for Further Reading

Blackorby, Edward C. *Prairie Populist: The Life and Times of Usher L. Burdick*, Janet Daley, editor. Fargo, ND: Institute for Regional Studies, 2001.

Brown, Patrick J. editor, *The People Celebrate: A Report on North Dakota's Centennial.* n.p., n.d..

A Century on the Northern Plains: The University of North Dakota at 100 Grand Forks: University of North Dakota Press, 1983.

Compendium of History and Biography of North Dakota. Chicago: George A. Ogle and Company, 1900.

Cooper, Jerry with Glenn Smith, *Citizens as Soldiers: A History of the North Dakota National Guard.* Lincoln: University of Nebraska Press, 1986.

Corcoran, James. *Bitter Harvest: Gordon Kahl and the Posse Comitatus: Murder in the Heartland.* New York: Penguin, 1990.

Cox, Wendell and Jean Love, *The Best Investment a Nation Ever Made: A Tribute to the Dwight D. Eisenhower System of Interstate and Defense Highways.* American Highway Users Alliance, Inc., 1998.

Crawford, Lewis F. *History of North Dakota.* Chicago: American Historical Society, 1931.

Davidson, Osha Gray. *Broken Heartland: The Rise of America's Rural Ghetto.* New York: The Free Press, 1990.

Fargo Forum.

Federal Writer's Project of the Works Progress Administration for the State of North Dakota. *North Dakota: A Guide of the Northern Prairie State.* Fargo: Knight Printing Company, 1938.

"Final Draft of the Constitutional Convention as Presented Thursday, February 17, 1972 to the Plenary Session." Bismarck: *Bismarck Tribune*, 1972.

Fink, Deborah. *Cutting into the Meatpacking Line: Workers and Change in the Rural Midwest.* Chapel Hill: University of North Carolina Press, 1998.

----------. *Open Country Iowa: Rural Women, Tradition and Change* Albany: State University of New York, 1986.

Fuller, John F. "Trial by Controversy: The Evolution of American Air Power From Birth to North Dakota." Unpublished M.A. Thesis, University of North Dakota, 1966.

Gardner, Bruce L. *American Agriculture in the Twentieth Century: How it Flourished and What it Cost.* Cambridge: Harvard University Press, 2002.

Geiger, Louis G. *University of the Northern Plains: A History of the University of North Dakota, 1883–1958.* Grand Forks: University of North Dakota Press, 1958.

Goodman, Lowell R. *The Economic Health of North Dakota.* Grand Forks, ND: LRG Properties, Ltd., 1996.

Graf, Darrell and Steve Schnabel, *It's All About Power: A True and Accurate Eye-Witness Account of the Shoot-out Between Gordon Kahl and US Marshals at Medina, North Dakota.* Fargo: MPD, Inc., 1999.

Grand Forks Herald.

Grand Forks Herald, *Come Hell and High Water: The Incredible Story of the 1997 Red River Flood.* Grand Forks: Grand Forks Herald, 1997.

Great Plains Institute for Sustainable Development. *Renewing the Countryside: North Dakota.* Minneapolis: Great Plains Institute for Sustainable Development/Northern Great Plains, Inc., 2003.

Guy, William L. "The Builder: William L. Guy," edited Gerald G. Newborg, *North Dakota History*, Vol. 71, 1 and 2 (2004).

Guy, William L. *Where Seldom Was Heard a Discouraging Word . . . Bill Guy Remembers.* Fargo, ND: Institute for Regional Studies, 1992.

Hagerty, Frank H. *The Territory of Dakota, the State of North Dakota, the State of South Dakota: An Official Statistical, Historical and Political Abstract.* Aberdeen, South Dakota: Aberdeen Daily News, 1889.

Harrison, Samuel S. and John P. Bluemle, *Flooding in the Grand Forks-East Grand Forks Area*, Educational Series 12, North Dakota Geological Survey. Fargo: Richtman's Incorporated, 1980.

Haugeberg, Karissa A. "A Legal Response to Legislative Failure: *ARC v North Dakota*." Honors Thesis, University of North Dakota, 2000.

Howe, Neil D. and Theodore B. Jelliff, *North Dakota: Legendary.* Fargo, ND: North Dakota Center for Distance Education, 2007.

Hurt, R. Douglas. *Agriculture: A Brief History.* Ames: Iowa State University Press, 1994.

Isern, Tom. *Dakota Circle: Excursions on the True Plains.* Fargo: Institute for Regional Studies, 2000.

Jelliff, Theodore B. *North Dakota: A Living Legacy.* Fargo: Kaye's and Knight Printing, 1983.

Junker, Rozanne Enerson. *The Bank of North Dakota: An Experiment in State Ownership.* Santa Barbara, CA: Fithian Press, 1989.

Kurian, Priya A. and Robert V. Bartlett, "The Garrison Diversion Dream and the Politics of Landscape Engineering." *North Dakota History* 59.3 (Summer 1992): 40–51.

Lam, James. "Evaluating the Impact of Federal Welfare Reform Legislation in Indian Country: A Policy Guide for the Standing Rock Sioux Tribe." Cambridge, MA: Harvard, May 1997.

Leifur, Conrad W. *Our State North Dakota.* New York: American Book Company, 1942.

Lewis, Tom. *Divided Highways: Building the Interstate Highways, Transforming American Life.* New York: Penguin, 1997.

Lounsberry, Clement A. *North Dakota: History and People, Outlines of American History*, Vols. 3. Chicago: S.J. Clarke Publishing, 1917.

MacGregor, Gordon. "Attitudes of the Fort Berthold Indians Regarding Removal from the Garrison Reservoir Site and Future Administration of Their Reservation." *North Dakota History*, 16.1 (1949): 31–60.

Marquart, Debra. *The Horizontal World: Growing Up Wild in the Middle of Nowhere.* New York: Counterpoint, 2006.

Nelson, Bruce, *Land of the Dacotahs.* Minneapolis: University of Minnesota Press, 1946.

Newgard, Thomas P., William C. Sherman and John Guerrero, *African Americans in North Dakota: Sources and Assessments.* Bismarck, North Dakota: University of Mary Press, 1995.

Nordin, Dennis S. and Roy V. Scott, *From Prairie Farmer to Entrepreneur: The Transformation of Midwestern Agriculture.* Bloomington: Indiana University Press, 2005.

Norris, Kathleen. *Dakota: A Spiritual Geography.* New York: Ticknor and Fields, 1993.

North Dakota Agricultural Statistics Service. Assorted reports.

North Dakota Blue Book. Various issues. Various schedules.

North Dakota State Data Center. Assorted reports.

Omdahl, Lloyd B. *Insurgents*. Brainerd, MN: Lakeland Color Press, 1961.

Popper, Deborah Epstein and Frank J. Popper, "The Great Plains: From Dust to Dust," *Planning* 53 (12, December 1987): 12–18.

Porter, Kimberly K. *Uncommon Heroes: The City of Grand Forks Flood Fight, 1997*. Grand Forks: North Dakota Museum of Art, 2001.

Rand, Kathryn R.L. and Steven Andrew Light, *Indian Gaming Law and Policy*. Durham, NC: Carolina Academic Press, 2006.

Rathke, Ann M. "Lady, If You Go Into Politics: North Dakota's Women Legislators, 1923–1989." Unpublished M.A. Thesis. University of North Dakota, 1990.

Rathke, Ann. "The Image of North Dakota in Recent American Travel Literature," *North Dakota Quarterly* 56.4 (Fall 1988): 86–98.

Remele, Larry. "North Dakota's Changing History." *North Dakota Quarterly* 56.4 (Fall 1988): 284–293.

Robinson, Elwyn B. *History of North Dakota*. Lincoln: University of Nebraska Press, 1966.

----------. "Six Themes of North Dakota History." *North Dakota History* 20.1 (Winter 1959): 5–24.

Rolfsrud, Erling Nicholai. *The Story of North Dakota*. Alexandria, MN: Lantern Books, 1963.

Rosenfeld, Harvey. *Roger Maris: A Title to Fame*. Fargo: Prairie House, 1991.

Russell, Brian K. "Flooded Lifeways: A Study of the Garrison Dam and Its Environmental Impact upon the Three Affiliated Tribes of the Fort Berthold Indian Reservation." Unpublished M.A. Essay. University of North Dakota, 2000.

Schardin, Justin "The HPR Governor Series: Gov. George Sinner, 1985–1992." *High Plains Reader*, November 11, 2007, 8–9.

Schneider, Mary Jane. *North Dakota Indians: An Introduction*. Dubuque, Iowa: Kendall/Hunt, 1986.

Sevareid, Eric *Not So Wild a Dream: A Personal Story of Youth and War and the American Faith*. New York: Knopf, 1946.

Shoptaugh Terry L. *Roots of Success: History of the Red River Valley Sugarbeet Growers*. Fargo: North Dakota Institute for Regional Studies, 1997.

Silberman, Robert *The Promise of the Politics of Water: The Garrison Diversion Project*. Fargo: North Dakota Institute for Regional Studies, 2002.

State of North Dakota, State Canvassing Board. Assorted abstracts.

Stern, Kenneth S. *A Force Upon the Plain: The American Militia Movement and the Politics of Hate*. New York: Simon and Schuster, 1996.

Stock, Catherine McNicol. *Rural Radicals: From Bacon's Rebellion to the Oklahoma City Bombing*. .New York: Penguin, 1996.

Stradley, Scot Arthur. *The Broken Circle: An Economic History of North Dakota*. Grand Forks, ND: Bureau of Business and Economic Research, 1993.

Streibel, Bryce. *Pathways Through Life: An Autobiography by Bryce Streibel*. Grand Forks, ND: The University of North Dakota Press, 1983.

Tauxe, Caroline S. *Farms, Mines and Main Streets: Uneven Development in a Dakota County*. Philadelphia: Temple University Press, 1993.

Taylor, Fred R. "North Dakota Agriculture Since World War II." *North Dakota History* 34.1 (Winter 1967): 47–61.

They Came to Stay: Grand Forks North Dakota Centennial, 1874– 1974. Grand Forks, North Dakota: Jet Printing, 1974.

Turner, Capstan with Jay Lowery, *There Was a Man: The Saga of Gordon Kahl: A True Story*. Nashville, TN: Sozo Publishing, 1995.

Tweton, D. Jerome. "Preface to the North Dakota Edition: Elwyn Robinson and the Themes of North Dakota History," Elwyn B. Robinson, *History of North Dakota*. Fargo: Institute for Regional Studies, North Dakota State University, 1994.

Tweton, D. Jerome and Theodore B. Jelliff. *North Dakota: The Heritage of a People*. Fargo: North Dakota Institute for Regional Studies, 1983.

United States Bureau of the Census. Various years. Various schedules. United States Department of Agriculture, National Agricultural Statistics Service. Assorted reports.

VanDevelder, Paul. *Coyote Warrior: One Man, Three Tribes, and the Trial that Forged a Nation*. New York: Little, Brown, 2004.

Wellentin, Loretta "Women and the United States Military: Achieving a Permanent Place." Unpublished M.A. Essay, University of North Dakota, 2006.

Wilkins, Robert P. and Wynona Huchette Wilkins, *North Dakota: A Bicentennial History*. The United States and the Nation Series, James Morton Smith, general editor. New York: W.W. Norton, 1977.

Wilkins, Wyonna H. "The Idea of North Dakota," *North Dakota Quarterly*, 39.1 (Winter 1971): 5–28.

Woiwode, Larry *Aristocrat of the West: The Story of Harold Schafer* Fargo: Institute for Regional Studies, 2000.

Wright, Boyd L. "North Dakota Votes" Bureau of Governmental Affairs, Special Report, #8. Grand Forks, ND: University of North Dakota, 1969.

Young, Allan C. "Race of the Century: Guy vs. Young, 1974 North Dakota U.S. Senate Election." Unpublished M.A. Thesis. University of North Dakota, 1989.

Endnotes

1 Elwyn B. Robinson, "The Themes of North Dakota History," revision of 75th Anniversary address, www.und.nodak.edu/dept/library/Collections/Robinson/themes.html, retrieved July 23, 2007.

2 Elywn B. Robinson, "Six Themes of North Dakota History," *North Dakota History* 20.1 (Winter 1959): 5–24.

3 D. Jerome Tweton, "Preface to the North Dakota Edition: Elwyn Robinson and the Themes of North Dakota History," Elwyn B. Robinson, *History of North Dakota* (Fargo: Institute for Regional Studies, North Dakota State University, 1994).

4 Ibid.

5 Quoted in ibid. See as well, Larry Remele, "North Dakota's Changing History," *North Dakota Quarterly* 56.4 (Fall 1988): 284–293.

6 Frank H. Hagerty, *The Territory of Dakota, the State of North Dakota, the State of South Dakota: An Official Statistical, Historical and Political Abstract* (Aberdeen, South Dakota: Aberdeen Daily News, 1889).

7 *Compendium of History and Biography of North Dakota* (Chicago: George A. Ogle and Company, 1900).

8 Clement A. Lounsberry, *North Dakota: History and People, Outlines of American History*, Vols. 3 (Chicago: S.J. Clarke Publishing, 1917.)

9 Ibid., vii.

10 Lewis F. Crawford, *History of North Dakota* (Chicago: American Historical Society, 1931); Federal Writer's Project of the Works Progress Administration for the State of North Dakota, *North Dakota: A Guide of the Northern Prairie State* (Fargo: Knight Printing Company, 1938).

11 See Conrad W. Leifur, *Our State North Dakota* (New York: American Book Company, 1942), Bruce Nelson, *Land of the Dacotahs* (Minneapolis: University of Minnesota Press, 1946), Erling Nicholai Rolfsrud, *The Story of North Dakota* (Alexandria, MN: Lantern Books, 1963). To be utterly fair about the matter, Nelson, Leifur and Rolfsrud did not perceive their works to be scholarly, but rather aimed their labors at the secondary classroom, or "for growing-up youngsters and for tired adults who like to read after a day of work" (Rolfsrud, 275). Perhaps no challenge to the interpretive framework had been intended.

12 Remele, 287; D. Jerome Tweton and Theodore B. Jelliff, *North Dakota: The Heritage of a People* (Fargo: North Dakota Institute for Regional Studies, 1976).

13 Tweton and Jelliff, Robert P. Wilkins and Wynnona H. Wilkins, *North Dakota: A History* (New York: W.W. Norton, 1977); Wilkins and Wilkins, xi–xii.

14 Theodore B. Jelliff, *North Dakota: A Living Legacy* (Fargo: Kaye's and Knight Printing, 1983).

15 Thomas P. Newgard, William C. Sherman and John Guerrero, *African Americans in North Dakota: Sources and Assessments* (Bismarck, North Dakota: University of Mary Press, 1995); William Guy, *Where Seldom was Heard a Discouraging Word ... Bill Guy Remembers* (Fargo: Institute for Regional Studies, 1992); Larry Woiwode, *Aristocrat of the West: The Story of Harold Schafer* (Fargo: Institute for Regional Studies, 2000); Harvey Rosenfeld, *Roger*

Maris: A Title to Fame (Fargo: Prairie House, 1991); Caroline S. Tauxe, *Farms, Mines and Main Streets: Uneven Development in a Dakota County* (Philadelphia: Temple University Press, 1993); James Corcoran, *Bitter Harvest: Gordon Kahl and the Posse Comitatus: Murder in the Heartland* (New York: Penguin, 1990); etc. Much work remains to be done on the state's heritage and no serious scholar can fail for want of a topic: oil industry, tourism, state bank, state mill and elevator, water issues, etc.

16 Elwyn B. Robinson, *History of North Dakota* (Lincoln: University of Nebraska Press, 1966), xv, passim.

17 See for example Tweton's *North Dakota: The Heritage of a People* (Fargo: North Dakota Institute for Regional Studies, 1983); *The Marquis de Morés: Dakota Capitalist, French Nationalist* (Fargo: North Dakota Institute for Regional Studies, 1972); *Grand Forks: A Pictorial History* (Norfolk: Donning Co., 1986); and with Daniel F. Rylance, *The Years of Despair: North Dakota in the Depression* (Grand Forks: Oxcart Press, 1973).

18 Tweton, "Preface to the North Dakota Edition: Elwyn Robinson and the Themes of North Dakota History," Elwyn Robinson, *History of North Dakota*, 2nd edition (Fargo: Institute for Regional Studies, 1995), xi.

19 Robinson, 136.

20 Robinson, 273–74.

21 Robinson, 407; see as well Ann Marie Low, *Dust Bowl Diary* (Lincoln: University of Nebraska Press, 1984).

22 Robinson, 407.

23 In the 1932 election, Roosevelt carried the state by over 100,000 votes when running against Herbert Hoover, and in the 1936 election the margin narrowed slightly to 90,000 votes when running against Alfred Landon.

24 Robinson, 415, 440; North Dakota Secretary of State, comp., "Official Abstract of Votes Cast at the General Election Held November 5, 1940," *Compilation of Election Returns National and State 1930–1944* (Bismarck, 1945); North Dakota Secretary of State, comp., "Official Abstract of Votes Cast at the General Election Held November 7, 1944," *Compilation of Election Returns National and State 1930–1944* (Bismarck, 1945).

25 Robinson, 429; see as well Loretta Wellentin, "Women and the United States Military: Achieving a Permanent Place," unpublished M.A. Essay, University of North Dakota, 2006.

26 Robinson, 429.

27 Robinson, 425; Tweton and Jelliff, 165.

28 Robinson, 425.

29 Robinson, 425.

30 Robinson, 427.

31 Louis G. Geiger, *University of the Northern Plains: A History of the University of North Dakota, 1883–1958* (Grand Forks: University of North Dakota Press, 1958), 401.

32 Tweton and Jelliff, 164.

33 John F. Fuller, "The New Look, Air Power, and North Dakota," *North Dakota Quarterly* 35.1 (Winter 1967): 1. The estimate held that the Soviets were at least 18 years, or six aircraft generations behind the United States in technological development.

34 Fuller, 2. For a more detailed examination of the arrival of Grand Forks and Minot Air Force Bases, see John F. Fuller, "Trial by Controversy: The Evolution of American Air Power From Birth to North Dakota," unpublished M.A. thesis, University of North Dakota, 1966, as well

as Rich Nolan, "The Air Force Comes to North Dakota: A Study in the Site Selection of Grand Forks and Minot Air Force Bases," unpublished M.A. thesis, University of North Dakota, 1990.

35 Fuller, "The New Look," 4.

36 Fuller, "The Air Force Comes to North Dakota," 36; Fuller, "A New Look," 8.

37 Fuller, "A New Look," 6.

38 Ibid., 5–7.

39 Ibid., 9.

40 "Minot Air Force Base—History," http://www.minot.af.mil/library/history.asp, retrieved August 22, 2007.

41 Fuller, "A New Look," 11–12; Office of History, "History of Grand Forks Air Force Base and the 319th Air Refueling Wing," (Grand Forks Air Force Base, 2003), 4.

42 Office of History, "History of Grand Forks Air Force Base," 4, 9.

43 Robinson, 462.

44 Robinson, 462; Ralph N. Shane, "A Short History of the Fort Berthold Indian Reservation," *North Dakota History* 26.4 (Fall 1959): 212–214; Patrick Springer, "A Flood of Tears: Five Decades Later, Tribes Still Recovering from Dam Losses," *Fargo Forum*, June 8, 2003. See as well, Gordon MacGregor, "Attitudes of the Fort Berthold Indians Regarding Removal from the Garrison Reservoir Site and Future Administration of Their Reservation," *North Dakota History*, 16.1 (1949): 31–60.

45 Springer; Shane, 212–214; see as well, Paul VanDevelder, *Coyote Warrior: One Man, Three Tribes, and the Trial that Forged a Nation* (New York: Little, Brown, 2004) and Brian K. Russell, "Flooded Lifeways: A Study of the Garrison dam and Its Environmental Impact upon the Three Affiliated Tribes of the Fort Berthold Indian Reservation," unpublished M.A. essay, University of North Dakota, 2000.

46 Springer.

47 Tweton and Jelliff, 179–181. Also impacting North Dakotans, and a product of the Pick-Sloan Flood Control Act of 1944, was the Oahe Dam constructed in central South Dakota just north of Pierre on the Missouri River. Begun in 1948 and dedicated on August 17, 1962, by President John F. Kennedy, the dam created Lake Oahe. Stretching some 230 miles north of the actual dam, the lake comes near to touching Bismarck, and provides both electric power and recreational opportunities for residents of both states. However, along the way to creating these opportunities, the entirety of Standing Rock Indian Reservation lost 55,944 acres of land to the lake, including 190 domestic water systems, 50 ranch water systems, 95 miles of main roads, 190 housing units, three sawmills, and the majority of the North Dakota side's prime agricultural land. Standing Rock Indian Reservation is predominantly home to Lakota and Dakota peoples. See United States Army Corps of Engineers, " Corps Lakes Gateway: South Dakota, Lake History," http://corpslakes.usace.army.mil/visitors/projects.cfm?Id=G612960, retrieved December 17, 2007. The reservation straddles the North Dakota/South Dakota state border. Of the reservation's 2,247,000 acres, 686,000 are in North Dakota and 1,561,000 are in South Dakota. "Standing Rock Sioux Tribe: Community Profile," http://www.mnisose.org/profiles/strock.htm, retrieved December 17, 2007.

48 Robinson, 535–36; Bill Snyder, "'Adding Picture to Sound'" Early Television in North Dakota," *North Dakota History* 60.3 (Summer 1993): 18.

[49] Robinson, 453, 455–58; see as well Wendell Cox and Jean Love, *The Best Investment a Nation Ever Made: A Tribute to the Dwight D. Eisenhower System of Interstate and Defense Highways* (American Highway Users Alliance, Inc., 1998) and Tom Lewis, *Divided Highways: Building the Interstate Highways, Transforming American Life* (New York: Penguin, 1997).

[50] Robinson, 458–59.

[51] Robinson, 460.

[52] Bryce Streibel, *Pathways Through Life: An Autobiography by Bryce Streibel* (Grand Forks, ND: The University of North Dakota Press, 1983), 79, 195–97.

[53] Robinson, 443.

[54] For a detailed accounting of the ROC, the Old Guard and the Insurgents, see Lloyd B. Omdahl, *Insurgents* (Brainerd, MN: Lakeland Color Press, 1961).

[55] Robinson, 470; Edward C. Blackorby, *Prairie Populist: The Life and Times of Usher L. Burdick*, Janet Daley, editor (Fargo, ND: Institute for Regional Studies, 2001), 297, 247, 278, 318–23, and 337, examines the life of Usher Burdick, particularly his struggles with the Republican party when at heart he most probably, in a two-party state, would have been cast as a Democratic contender.

[56] *Time*, "The Partisan League," April 9, 1956.

[57] Robinson, 470–71.

[58] Ibid.; "Presidential General Election Results Comparison—North Dakota," http://www.uselectionatlas.org/RESULTS/compare.php?year=1956&fips+38&f=0&off, retrieved December 5, 2007.

[59] Robinson, 473.

[60] United States Bureau of the Census, *U.S. Census of Population: 1960*. Vol. I, Characteristics of the Population, Part 36, North Dakota. (Washington, D.C.: U.S. Government Printing Office, 1963), Table 1—"Population of the State, Urban and Rural: 1870–1960," 36–9. The population of North Dakota in 1960 was predominantly white. Less than 2 percent recorded themselves as "nonwhite" which was undifferentiated as to Native American, African American, Asian American, etc. See, ibid., Table 14, "Color by Sex, for the State, by size of Place, 1960, and Urban and Rural Residence, 1960," 36–28.

[61] Robinson, *History of North Dakota*, 443; for an example of youth leaving North Dakota in the late 1940s see Bryce Streibel, *Pathways Through Life: An Autobiography of Bryce Streibel* (Grand Forks, ND: University of North Dakota Press, 1983).

[62] Robinson, 443; see Streibel as well for a discussion of elders leaving the state for warmer climates.

[63] Ibid.; Fred R. Taylor, "North Dakota Agriculture Since World War II," *North Dakota History* 34.1 (Winter 1967): 58.

[64] United States Bureau of the Census, *U.S. Census of Population: 1960*. Vol. I, Characteristics of the Population, Part 36, North Dakota. (Washington, D.C.: U.S. Government Printing Office, 1963), Table 6—"Area and Population of Counties, Urban and Rural: 1960 and 1950," 36–12.

[65] Ibid.; Robinson, 443; Taylor, 58.

[66] United States Bureau of the Census, *U.S. Census of Population: 1960*. Vol. I, Characteristics of the Population, Part 36, North Dakota. (Washington, D.C.: U.S. Government Printing Office, 1963), Table 57-"Occupation Group of Employed Persons, by Sex for the State, Urban and Rural: 1960," 36–135.

[67] National Oceanic and Atmospheric Administration, "Climate at a Glance: Annual Precipitation: North Dakota," http://climvis.ncdc.noaa.gov/ccgi-bin/cag3/hr-display3.pl, retrieved November 29, 2007; William L. Guy, "The Builder: William L. Guy," edited Gerald G. *Newborg, North Dakota History,* Vol. 71, 1 and 2 (2004): 31.

[68] R. Douglas Hurt, *Agriculture: A Brief History* (Ames: Iowa State University Press, 1994), 354–55.

[69] Taylor, 54–56.

[70] Ibid. Average "farm" size is somewhat misleading as it includes farms as well as ranches.

[71] Ibid., 57.

[72] Robinson, 453.

[73] United States Department of Agriculture, National Agricultural Statistics Service, "USDA Historical Track Records," (Washington, D.C.: United States Government Printing Office, 2005), 131, 140.

[74] Ibid., 19, 115–16.

[75] Cattle Fax, "Omaha Prices: Fat Steers, 1940–2007," http://cattle-fax.com/files/beef/omahasprices.xls, retrieved December 20, 2007.

[76] Boyd L. Wright, "North Dakota Votes" Bureau of Governmental Affairs, Special Report, #8 (Grand Forks, ND: University of North Dakota, 1969), 41.

[77] William L. Guy, *Where Seldom Was Heard a Discouraging Word . . . Bill Guy Remembers* (Fargo, ND: Institute for Regional Studies, 1992), 47–51.

[78] Boyd L. Wright, "North Dakota Votes" Bureau of Governmental Affairs, Special Report, #8 (Grand Forks, ND: University of North Dakota, 1969), 42; *Grand Forks Herald*, June 28, 1960, and June 30, 1960.

[79] Woodrow Wilson carried the state twice, 1912 and 1916, and Franklin D. Roosevelt carried the state twice as well, 1932 and 1936.

[80] "Presidential General Election Results Comparison-North Dakota," http://www.uselectionalas.org/RESULTS/compare.php?year=1956&fips=38&f=0&off=0, retrieved December 5, 2007.

[81] Guy, "The Builder," 33, 26.

[82] Neil D. Howe and Theodore B. Jelliff, *North Dakota: Legendary* (Fargo, ND: North Dakota Center for Distance Education, 2007), 324.

[83] Robinson, 455–58; State Historical Society of North Dakota, "Chronology of North Dakota," 1960, http://www.state.nd.us/hist/chrono.htm, retrieved May 6, 2006.

[84] Nearly 800 North Dakota National Guardsmen from throughout the state met the call to service in West Germany to demonstrate to the Soviets the determination of Americans to maintain Berlin's integrity. Bismarck, Minot, Rugby, Mott, Linton, Williston and Grand Forks units spent approximately ten months in Germany. See Jerry Cooper, with Glenn Smith, *Citizens as Soldiers: A History of the North Dakota National Guard* (Lincoln: University of Nebraska Press, 1986), 404–06.

[85] Minot Air Force Base, "History," http://www.minot.af.mil/library/history.asp, retrieved August 22, 2007.

[86] Global Security, "Weapons of Mass Destruction," http://www.globalsecurity.org/wmd/facility/minot/htm, retrieved December 5, 2007.

[87] Ibid.

[88] "Missile Silos,"*Dakota Datebook*, October 12, 2003, http://www.prairiepublic.org/programs/datebook/bydate/03/1003/101202.jsp, retrieved December 24, 2007.

[89] Office of History, "History of Grand Forks Air Force Base and the 319th Air Refueling Wing," (Grand Forks Air Force Base, 2003), 4.

[90] Ibid., 9.

[91] Robinson, 453.

[92] Ibid.

[93] Guy, "The Builder," 40–41; recipients in order of award, Welk (August 28, 1961), Stickney (November 2, 1961), Dmitri (April 13, 1962), Maris (January 4, 1964) Sevareid (April 17, 1964), General Harold K. Johnson, military service (April 23, 1965), Dr. Anne H. Carlsen, educator (September 9, 1966), Edward K. Thompson, journalist (April 19, 1968), Dr. Robert Henry Bahmer, archivist (July 28, 1970), Louis L'Amour, author (May 26, 1972), Bertin C. Gamble, entrepreneur (October 20, 1972), Caster Oimoen, athlete (February 1, 1973), Peggy Lee, entertainer (May 23, 1975), Harold Schafer, entrepreneur (July 4, 1975), Era Bell Thompson, journalist (August 14, 1976), Dr. Leon Orris Jacobson, physician (October 1, 1976), Elizabeth Bodine, humanitarian (July 27, 1979), Clifford "Fido" Purpur, athlete (May 16, 1981), Phyllis Frelich, actress (April 27, 1981), General David C. Jones, military service (May 21, 1982), Ronald N. Davies, judge (June 11, 1987), Phillip D. Jackson, athlete (July 30, 1992), Angie Dickinson, actress (December 2, 1992), Reverend Richard C. Halverson, minister (March 26, 1994), Brynhild Haugland, legislator (March 20, 1995), Admiral William A. Owens, military service (January 29, 1996), Carl Ben Eielson, pioneer aviator (August 26, 1997), Warren Christopher, public servant (June 20, 1998), Bobby Vee, entertainer (June 20, 1999), Chester "Chet" Reiten, entrepreneur (October 8, 2002), Thomas J. Clifford, entrepreneur (November 23, 2002), Sister Thomas Welder, educator (May 1, 2004), Harry J. Pearce, business leader (August 11, 2004), William C. Marcil, business leader (May 18, 2006), see http://www.governor.state.nd.us/awards/rr-gallery/toc.html, retrieved December 24, 2007.

[94] Guy, "The Builder," 31, 41–42.

[95] Guy, "The Builder," 42, 36.

[96] Ibid.; see as well, Ben Meier, Secretary of State, *North Dakota Blue Book, 1961* (Bismarck, ND: *Bismarck Tribune*, 1961), 99, and Ben Meier, Secretary of State, *North Dakota Blue Book, 1973* (n.p., n.d.), 120.

[97] Guy, "The Builder," 36–37. See Guy as well for a detailed accounting of his difficulties with A.J. Jensen, state insurance commissioner, with regard to accountability for state funds, 36–37.

[98] Quoted in Rozanne Enerson Junker, *The Bank of North Dakota: An Experiment in State Ownership* (Santa Barbara: Fithian Press, 1989), 139.

[99] Ibid., 140–41.

[100] Ibid., 143.

[101] "Leland Olds Station," http://www.basinelectric.com/EnergyResources/electricity/BaseLoad/LOS.html, retrieved December 31, 2007; Guy, *Where Never Was Heard a Discouraging Word.*

[102] Robinson, 455.

[103] Boyd L. Wright, "North Dakota Votes" Bureau of Governmental Affairs, Special Report, #8 (Grand Forks, ND: University of North Dakota, 1969), 42–43.

[104] Ben Meier, Secretary of State, *North Dakota Centennial Blue Book, 1889–1989* (n.p., n.d.), 448; Boyd L. Wright, "North Dakota Votes" Bureau of Governmental Affairs, Special Report, #8 (Grand Forks, ND: University of North Dakota, 1969), 42–43.

105 National population figure from the 1965 *Information Please Almanac*, available at http://www.infoplease.com/year/1965.html, retrieved December 31, 2007; state population from the United States Department of Commerce, Bureau of the Census, Vol.I Characteristics of the Population, Part 36, North Dakota "North Dakota: Number of Inhabitants," (Washington, D.C.: United States Government Printing Office, 1972), 36–4, 5; Wilkins and Wilkins, 188.

106 Figures extrapolated from United States Department of Commerce, Bureau of the Census, Vol.I Characteristics of the Population, Part 36, North Dakota "North Dakota: Number of Inhabitants," (Washington, D.C.: United States Government Printing Office, 1972), 36–4, 5, 32–33 and United States Bureau of the Census, *U.S. Census of Population: 1960*. Vol. I, Characteristics of the Population, Part 36, North Dakota. (Washington, D.C.: U.S. Government Printing Office, 1963), Table I—Population of the State, Urban and Rural: 1870–1960, 36–9. See Robinson, 444–45; Hurt, 371–75.

107 United States Department of Agriculture, National Agricultural Statistics Service, "USDA Historical Track Records," (Washington, D.C.: United States Government Printing Office, 2005), 19, 131, 140, and 116.

108 Cattle Fax, "Omaha Prices: Fat Steers, 1940–2007," http://cattle-fax.com/files/beef/omahasprices.xls, retrieved December 20, 2007.

109 Taylor, 47–61.

110 United States Department of Agriculture, National Agricultural Statistics Service, "Farm Numbers—Total Farms, Land in Farms, Average Farm Size," http://www.nass.usda.gov/QuickStats/PullData_US.jsp, retrieved January 2, 2008; Taylor, 58.

111 National Oceanic and Atmospheric Administration, "Climate at a Glance: Annual Precipitation: North Dakota," http://climvis.ncdc.noaa.gov/ccgi-bin/cag3/hr-display3.pl, retrieved November 29, 2007.

112 Samuel S. Harrison and John P. Bluemle, *Flooding in the Grand Forks-East Grand Forks Area*, Educational Series 12, North Dakota Geological Survey (Fargo: Richtman's Incorporated, 1980), 17–18.

113 Ibid., 18.

114 For the best examination of the blizzard of 1966, see Douglas Ramsey and Larry Skroch, *One to Remember: The Relentless Blizzard of March 1966* (Grand Forks: Valley Heritage Press, 2004).

115 Ramsey and Skroch, 194.

116 Ibid., 222.

117 Ibid., 323.

118 *Minot Daily News*, "The Mighty Mouse River," http://pages.minot.k12.nd.us/nodak/flood/showNews.php?story=01, retrieved December 31, 2007.

119 United States Department of Agriculture, National Agricultural Statistics Service, "Farm Numbers—Total Farms, Land in Farms, Average Farm Size," http://www.nass.usda.gov/QuickStats/PullData_US.jsp, retrieved January 2, 2008.

120 "Leland Olds Station," http://www.basinelectric.com/EnergyResources/electricity/BaseLoad/LOS.html, retrieved December 31, 2007; Guy, "The Builders," 36.

121 Robinson, 460; "Oil Capital of North Dakota," http://tiogand.net/index.asp?type=B_BASIC&SEC={C4316BD-732-4E9F-B05E-81D1D49A4624}, retrieved September 4, 2007.

122 Terry L. Shoptaugh, *Roots of Success: History of the Red River Valley Sugarbeet Growers* (Fargo: North Dakota Institute for Regional Studies, 1997), 20–22.

123 Ibid., 79, 111.

124 Ibid., 130–32.

125 Robinson, 463.

126 Ibid.; see as well Vernon Cooper, "Garrison Diversion—A Project for All North Dakotans," *The North Dakota Quarterly* 35.3 (Summer 1967): 72–7.

127 Garrison Diversion, "Chronology," http://www.garrisondiv.org/pages/publicinfo/chronology/index.epl, retrieved January 3, 2008.

128 Robinson, 466.

129 Tweton and Jelliff, 181–82; Patrick Springer, "The Quest for Water," *The [Fargo] Forum*, http://www.in-forum.com/specials/century/jan3/week6.htm, retrieved January 3, 2008.

130 Tweton and Jelliff, 179; Wilkins and Wilkins, 188; "Missile Threat: Safeguard," http://missilethreat.com/missiledefensesystems/id.55/system_detail.asp, retrieved December 24, 2007.

131 Wilkins and Wilkins, 188.

132 Guy, *Where Seldom was Heard a Discouraging Word* 199–211.

133 "King of the Referendum," *Time*, June 13, 1977.

134 Ben Meier, Secretary of State, *North Dakota Centennial Blue Book, 1889–1989* (n.p., n.d.), 432–55.

135 Ibid.; "King of the Referendum," *Time*, June 13, 1977; Boyd L. Wright, "North Dakota Votes" Bureau of Governmental Affairs, Special Report, #8 (Grand Forks, ND: University of North Dakota, 1969), 46.

136 Boyd L. Wright, "North Dakota Votes" Bureau of Governmental Affairs, Special Report, #8 (Grand Forks, ND: University of North Dakota, 1969), 46.

137 United States Department of Commerce, Bureau of the Census, Vol.1 Characteristics of the Population, Part 36, North Dakota "North Dakota: Number of Inhabitants," (Washington, D.C.: United States Government Printing Office, 1972), 36–4, 5.

138 Between 1960 and 1970, the population of Tioga, center of the oil industry in North Dakota, dropped from 2,087 to 1,667, while that of Williston, also in the heart of the state's oil district dropped from 11,866 to 11,280. See *North Dakota Census at a Glance*, "City Population by County and Year, 1940 to 1990," (Fargo: North Dakota State University, 1993), 135–136.

139 United States Department of Agriculture, National Agricultural Statistics Service, "Farm Numbers—Total Farms, Land in Farms, Average Farm Size," http://www.nass.usda.gov/QuickStats/PullData_US.jsp, retrieved January 2, 2008; R. Douglas Hurt, *American Agriculture: A Brief History* (Ames: Iowa State University Press, 1994), 331–76.

140 Prairie Public, Dakota Datebook, May 10, 2004, "Zip to Zap," http://www.prairiepublic.org/programs/datebook/bydate/04/0504/051004.jsp, retrieved October 30, 2007.

141 Ibid.

142 Ibid.

143 Ibid.

[144] Ibid. See as well, Richard Shafer, "Spinning the Zip to Zap: Student Journalist Responsibility and Vulnerability in the Late 1960s," http://www2.edutech.nodakedu/ndsta/shafer.htm, retrieved October 30, 2007; Jack Sullivan, "Zap Overwhelmed as College Lark Turned to Chaos," *The* [Fargo] *Forum*, http://www.in-forum.com/specials/century/jan3/week9.htm, retrieved October 30, 2007; and Jerry Cooper with Glenn Smith, *Citizens as Soldiers: A History of the North Dakota National Guard* (Lincoln: University of Nebraska Press, 1986), 430–34.

[145] United States Bureau of the Census, *U.S. Census of Population: 1960*. Vol. I, Characteristics of the Population, Part 36, North Dakota, (Washington, D.C.: U.S. Government Printing Office, 1963), Table I—Population of the State, Urban and Rural: 1870–1960, 36–9; United States Department of Commerce, *1970 Census of Population*. Vol. I, "Characteristics of the Population," Part 36, North Dakota.(Washington, D.C.: United States Government Printing Office, 1973), 36–7.

[146] Ibid.

[147] United States Department of Commerce, *1970 Census of Population: Supplementary Report*, "1970 Population of North Dakota by County Subdivisions: 1970–1960," Part 36, North Dakota. (Washington, D.C.: United States Government Printing Office, 1976), 36-2-14.

[148] Ibid.

[149] United States Bureau of the Census, *1970 Census of the Population*, Characteristics of the Population, North Dakota, Part 36, Table 17, "Race by Sex: 1900–1970," 36–36.

[150] United States Department of Commerce, *1970 Census of Population: Supplementary Report*, "1970 Population of North Dakota by County Subdivisions: 1970–1960,"Part 36, North Dakota. (Washington, D.C.: United States Government Printing Office, 1976), 36-2-14.

[151] United States Bureau of the Census, "Table 1. Urban and Rural Population: 1900 to 1990," released October 1995, http://www.census.gov/population/censusdata/urpop0090.txt, retrieved January 20, 2008.

[152] United States Department of Agriculture, National Agricultural Statistics Service, "Total Farms, Land in Farms, Average Farm Size," http://www.nass.usda.gov/QuickStats/PullData_US.jsp, retrieved January 2, 2008; R. Douglas Hurt, *American Agriculture: A Brief History* (Ames: Iowa State University Press, 1994), 331–78.

[153] United States Department of Agriculture, National Agricultural Statistics Service, "USDA Historical Track Records," (Washington, D.C.: United States Government Printing Office, 2005), 131.

[154] Ibid., 140. The early 1970s were somewhat dry years for the state as a whole. The years 1971–74 all had precipitation less than average for the state's 17.6" fifty-year average. See National Oceanic and Atmospheric Administration, "Climate at a Glance: Annual Precipitation: North Dakota," http://climvis.ncdc.noaa.gov/ccgi-bin/cag3/hr-display3.pl, retrieved November 29, 2007.

[155] United States Department of Agriculture, National Agricultural Statistics Service, "USDA Historical Track Records," (Washington, D.C.: United States Government Printing Office, 2005), 19.

[156] Ibid., 116.

[157] Shoptaugh, 175–76.

[158] Cattle Fax, "Omaha Prices: Fat Steers, 1940–2007," http://cattle-fax.com/files/beef/omahasprices.xls, retrieved December 20, 2007.

[159] Dennis S. Nordin and Roy V. Scott, *From Prairie Farmer to Entrepreneur: The Transformation of Midwestern Agriculture* (Bloomington: Indiana University Press, 2005), 191–92.

[160] Jerome E. Johnson, "1974: Second Year of Sharp Farmland Value Increases," North Dakota Agricultural Experiment Station, Reprint No. 854, Vol. 32, No. 5, p.3.

[161] *Grand Forks Herald*, July 28, 1970; *They Came to Stay: Grand Forks North Dakota Centennial, 1874–1974* (Grand Forks, North Dakota: Jet Printing, 1974), 41–42.

[162] United States Bureau of the Census, *U.S. Census of Population: 1960*. Vol. I, Characteristics of the Population, Part 36, North Dakota. (Washington, D.C.: U.S. Government Printing Office, 1963), Table 7—"Population of Counties, by Minor Civil Divisions: 1940 to 1960," 36-19; United States Department of Commerce, *1970 Census of Population*. Vol. I, Characteristics of the Population, Part 36, North Dakota. (Washington, D.C.: United States Government Printing Office, 1973), Table 10-"Population of County Subdivisions: 1970 and 1960," 36–20. The annual production of oil, in terms of barrels, in 1960, stood at 21,993,603, rising slightly to 22,006,300 barrels per year in 1970, but declining to 20,452,740 in 1975, as the international price of oil declined. See, North Dakota Industrial Commission, Department of Mineral Resources, Alvin A. Jaeger, *North Dakota Blue Book, 1997–1999* (Bismarck, ND: n.p., 1997), 506–10.

[163] Ben Meier, Secretary of State, *North Dakota Centennial Blue Book, 1889–1989* (n.p., n.d.), 121. From 1913–1933, North Dakotans elected three districts of representatives. From 1933–1963, two representatives were elected at large to Congress, and from 1963 through 1972, two representatives were elected by district to the Congress. See *North Dakota Centennial Blue Book, 1889–1989*, 121–22.

[164] Ibid., 101–03.

[165] Ibid.

[166] George Sinner, Vice President, Board of Higher Education, "Report to the Committee on Budget of Legislative Council," February 18, 1970, President's Office Records, Collection UA #43, Box 30, University of North Dakota, Department of Special Collections, Grand Forks, ND; hereafter President's Office Records.

[167] Elywn B. Robinson, "The Themes of North Dakota History," revision of 75th Anniversary address,http://www.und.nodak/dept/library/Collections/Robinson/themes.html, accessed July 23, 2007.

[168] Sinner, p. 3; *Mandan* [North Dakota] *Pioneer*, January 11, 1970; "Requiem and Renewal," President's Office Records.

[169] Ben Meier, Secretary of State, *North Dakota Blue Book, 1973* (n.p., n.d.), 81.

[170] *A Century on the Northern Plains: The University of North Dakota at 100* (Grand Forks: University of North Dakota Press, 1983), 84.

[171] Ibid.

[172] Guy, *Where Seldom Was Heard a Discouraging Word* 93–94.

[173] Ibid., 94–95.

[174] Ibid.

[175] Ibid., 96–97.

[176] Cooper with Smith, 434–38.

[177] Ibid.; Guy, 96–98.

[178] Guy, 98.

179 United States Military Personnel Who Died (Including Missing and Captured Declared Dead) as a Result of the Vietnam Conflict, 1957–1995," http://www.archives.gov/research/vietnam-war/casualty-lists/nd-alpha.html, retrieved November 5, 2007.

180 Minot Air Force Base, "History," http://www.minot.af.mil/library/history.asp, retrieved August 22, 2007; Office of History, "History of Grand Forks Air Force Base and the 319th Air Refueling Wing," (Grand Forks Air Force Base, 2003), 5–6.

181 Priya A. Kurian and Robert V. Bartlett, "The Garrison Diversion Dream and the Politics of Landscape Engineering," *North Dakota History* 59.3 (Summer 1992): 40–51

182 Tweton and Jelliff, 176–77. See as well, Caroline S. Tauxe, *Farmers, Mines and Main Streets: Uneven Development in a Dakota County* (Philadelphia: Temple University Press, 1993).

183 "Final Draft of the Constitutional Convention as Presented Thursday, February 17, 1972 to the Plenary Session," (Bismarck: *Bismarck Tribune*, 1972), xiv–xv.

184 Ibid., xv.

185 Ibid.; Guy, "The Builder": 39.

186 Ben Meier, Secretary of State, *North Dakota Centennial Blue Book, 1889–1989* (n.p., n.d.), 121.

187 Guy, "The Builder," 39. See as well, Albert P Melone and Judson H. Jones, "Constitutional Convention Delegates and Interest Groups: A Panel Study of Elite Socialization," *The Journal of Politics*, 44.1 (February 1982): 182–92.

188 Arthur A. Link, "Guardian of the Land: Arthur A. Link," Gerald G. Newborg, editor, *North Dakota History*, 72. 1 and 2: 46.

189 "Arthur A. Link," North Dakota Governors, State Historical Society of North Dakota, http://www.nd.gov/hist/ndgov6.htm, retrieved July 27, 2007.

190 Meier, 120–22.

191 "North Dakota Votes," http://www.history.com/encyclopedia.do?articleid=226809, retrieved November 11, 2007.

192 Bureau of Governmental Affairs, University of North Dakota, "Vote of the People: A Brief History and Compilation of all Measures Submitted to a Vote of the People of North Dakota from Statehood through 1974," 35.

193 Kurt Vonnegut, "Kurt Vonnegut on Censorship and Moral Values," *Modern Fiction Studies*, Vol. 26.4. (1981), 683. See as well, Vonnegut, *Palm Sunday: An Autobiographical Collage* (New York: Dial Press, 1999), 1–16.

194 For a detailed examination of the 1974 senatorial race in North Dakota see Allan C. Young, "Race of the Century: Guy vs. Young, 1974 North Dakota U.S. Senate Election," M.A. thesis, University of North Dakota, 1989.

195 Guy, "The Builder," 44–45.

196 Young, 118.

197 Ben Meier, Secretary of State, *North Dakota Centennial Blue Book, 1889–1989* (n.p., n.d.), 120; United States Department of Agriculture, National Agricultural Statistics Service, "USDA Historical Track Records," (Washington, D.C.: United States Government Printing Office, 2005). OPEC's move to cut oil sales to the United States and to raise the price of oil sold elsewhere came as a result of the United States' support of Israel in the Yom Kippur War of 1973 when a devastating Syrian-Egyptian attack surprised the nation on the holiest day of the Jewish year; see George Brown Tindall and David E. Shi, *America: A Narrative History*, 4th Edition, Vol. 2 (New York: W.W. Norton, 1996), 1469.

[198] Bureau of Business and Economic Research, "North Dakota Crude Oil Production, 1951–1978," Table 9.05, *Statistical Abstract of North Dakota, 1979* (University of North Dakota: Grand Forks, 1979), 347.

[199] Ibid., 342; Ben Meier, Secretary of State, *North Dakota Centennial Blue Book, 1889–1989* (n.p., n.d.), 531.

[200] Bureau of Business and Economic Research, "North Dakota Crude Oil Production, 1951–1978," Table 9.05, *Statistical Abstract of North Dakota, 1979* (University of North Dakota: Grand Forks, 1979), 345; Ben Meier, Secretary of State, *North Dakota Centennial Blue Book, 1889–1989* (n.p., n.d.), 531.

[201] Bureau of Business and Economic Research, "Population of North Dakota State Planning Regions and SMSA's, Selected Years, 1950–1977," Table 1.03, *Statistical Abstract of North Dakota, 1979* (Grand Forks: University of North Dakota, 1979), 9.

[202] United States Department of Commerce, *1970 Census of Population.* Vol. I, Characteristics of the Population, Part 36, North Dakota. (Washington, D.C.: United States Government Printing Office, 1973), 36–7; United States Department of Commerce, *1980 Census of Population.* Vol. I, Characteristics of the Population, Part 36, North Dakota. (Washington, D.C.: United States Government Printing Office, 1983), 36–7. Percent extrapolated from statistical comparisons gathered from the above. See as well, "North Dakota Data—Farm Numbers—Total Farms, Land in Farms, Average Farm Size," http://www.nass.usda.gov/QuickStats/PullData_US.jsp, retrieved January 2, 2008.

[203] United States Department of Agriculture, National Agricultural Statistics Service, "USDA Historical Track Records," (Washington, D.C.: United States Government Printing Office, 2005), 131.

[204] Ibid., 140.

[205] Ibid., 19.

[206] Ibid., 116

[207] Ibid., 123; State Historical Society of North Dakota, "Chronology of North Dakota History—1978," http://www.state.nd.us/hist/chrono.htm, retrieved May 26, 2006.

[208] Cattle Fax, "Omaha Prices: Fat Steers, 1940–2007," http://www.cattle-fax.com/data/files/beef/omahastrprice.xls, retrieved December 20, 2007.

[209] United States Department of Agriculture, National Agricultural Statistics Service, "Total Farms, Land in Farms, Average Farm Size," http://www.nass.usda.gov/QuickStats/PullData_US.jsp, retrieved January 2, 2008. Percentage derived from the above tables divided by the state's 45,225,600 acres of surface area, inclusive of areas covered by water.

[210] Ibid.

[211] Jerome E. Johnson, "1979 Farmland Values," *Farm Research*, 37.5 (March-April 1980), 24; see R. Douglas Hurt, *American Agriculture: A Brief History* (Ames: Iowa State University Press, 1994), 331–76, for a discussion of the state of agriculture nationwide at this time, as well as for an understanding of the issues which were already in place to bring the farm crisis of the 1980s.

[212] *Grand Forks Herald*, January 10, 1975, 1 and 8; January 13, 1975, and 5.

[213] *Grand Forks Herald*, January 13, 1975, 1 and 5. Strangely, the nation also suffered a series of deadly tornadoes the same weekend. Forty-five confirmed tornadoes touched down in a band from Texas and Oklahoma to Florida and Georgia. A dozen individuals lost their

lives to the storms, with another 377 seriously injured. Initial estimates regarding damage ran to approximately $45 million.

214 Ibid.; *Grand Forks Herald*, January 15, 1975, 1.

215 *Grand Forks Herald*, January 17, 1975, 1.

216 *Grand Forks Herald*, December 30, 1975, 1.

217 Harrison and Bluemle, 19–20.

218 Ibid.

219 Ibid., National Oceanic and Atmospheric Administration, "Climate at a Glance: Annual Precipitation: North Dakota," http://climvis.ncdc.noaa.gov/ccgi-bin/cag3/hr-display3.pl, retrieved November 29, 2007.

220 Ibid., 21–22.

221 Ibid., 22–24.

222 United States Military Personnel Who Died (Including Missing and Captured Declared Dead) as a Result of the Vietnam Conflict, 1957–1995," http://www.archives.gov/research/vietnam-war/casualty-lists/nd-alpha.html, retrieved November 5, 2007.

223 Ibid.; Tindall and Shi, 1464

224 Tweton and Jelliff, 179; Wilkins and Wilkins, 188; "Missile Threat: Safeguard," http://missilethreat.com/missiledefensesystems/id.55/system_detail.asp, retrieved December 24, 2007.

225 GlobalSecurity.org, "Weapons of Mass Destruction: Stanley R. Mickelsen Safeguard Complex," http://www.globalsecurity.org/wmd/facility/mickelsen.htm, retrieved December 24, 2007.

226 Ibid.

227 Stanley R. Mickelsen Safeguard Complex, "Introduction," http://www.srmsc.org/intl000/html, retrieved December 24, 2007.

228 Ibid.; quoted in "Phase-Out/Abandonment of the SRMSC," http://www.srmsc.org/int2070.html, retrieved December 24, 2007.

229 Ibid., *Grand Forks Herald*, December 30, 1975, 1.

230 University of Mary, "Arthur A. Link and Grace Johnson Link," http://www.umary.edu/UM/News/linkbios.htm, retrieved January 7, 2008.

231 Quoted in Link, "Guardian of the Land: Arthur A. Link," 46.

232 Ibid., 25.

233 Ibid.

234 Link, 24–26.

235 Link, 27.

236 Tweton and Jelliff, 196–97.

237 Ann M. Rathke, "Lady, If You Go Into Politics: North Dakota's Women Legislators, 1923–1989," unpublished M.A. Essay, University of North Dakota, 1990; David B. Danbom, "Postscript," Elwyn B. Robinson, *History of North Dakota* (Lincoln: University of Nebraska Press, 1966), Institute for Regional Studies (1995), 584, 591.

238 Rathke, 199–200.

239 State of North Dakota, State Canvassing Board, "Official Abstract of Votes Cast at the General Election Held November 2, 1976"; William A. DeGregorio, *The Complete Book of U.S. Presidents: From Washington to Bill Clinton*, 4th edition (New York: Wings Books, 1993), 623–24.

240 Link, 37.

241 State of North Dakota, State Canvassing Board, "Official Abstract of Votes Cast at the General Election Held November 2, 1976".

242 Link, 25–27.

243 Initiative and Referendum Institute, "North Dakota," http://www.iandrinstitute.org/North%20Dakota.htm, retrieved December 7, 2007.

244 Patrick Springer, "The Quest for Water," *Fargo Forum*, http://www.in-forum.com/specials/century/jan3/week6.htm, retrieved January 3, 2008.

245 Ibid.; see as well Robert Silberman, *The Promise of the Politics of Water: The Garrison Diversion Project* (Fargo: North Dakota Institute for Regional Studies, 2002).

246 Rozanne Enerson Junker, *The Bank of North Dakota: An Experiment in State Ownership* (Santa Barbara, CA: Fithian Press, 1989), 138–58.

247 United States Department of Commerce, *1980 Census of Population*. Vol. I, Characteristics of the Population, Part 36, North Dakota. (Washington, D.C.: United States Government Printing Office, 1983), Table 1, "Population of the State: Earliest Census to 1980," Table 2, "Land Area and Population: 1930–1980," 36-5-8.

248 Ibid.

249 United States Department of Commerce, *1980 Census of Population*. Vol. I, Characteristics of the Population, Part 36, North Dakota. (Washington, D.C.: United States Government Printing Office, 1983), Table 15, "Persons by Race: 1980", 36–10 and Table 16, "Total Persons and Spanish Origin Persons by Type of Spanish Origin and Race: 1980," 36–12.

250 United States Department of Commerce, *1980 Census of Population*. Vol. I, Characteristics of the Population, Part 36, North Dakota. (Washington, D.C.: United States Government Printing Office, 1983), Table 217, "Detailed Occupation of the Experienced Civilian Labor Force and Employed Person by Sex: 1980 and 1970," 36–56.

251 Ibid., Rathke; David B. Danbom, "Postscript," Elwyn B. Robinson, *History of North Dakota* (Lincoln: University of Nebraska Press, 1966), Institute for Regional Studies (1995), 584, 591.

252 United States Department of Commerce, *1980 Census of Population*. Vol. I, Characteristics of the Population, Part 36, North Dakota. (Washington, D.C.: United States Government Printing Office, 1983), Table 217, "Detailed Occupation of the Experienced Civilian Labor Force and Employed Person by Sex: 1980 and 1970," 36-56-64.

253 Jerome E. Johnson, "Farmland Values Declined More in 1984," North Dakota Farm Research, Vol. 43.4 (January-February 1985), 7.

254 Ibid.

255 United States Department of Agriculture, National Agricultural Statistics Service, "Total Farms, Land in Farms, Average Farm Size," http://www.nass.usda.gov/QuickStats/PullData_US.jsp, retrieved January 2, 2008.

256 United States Department of Agriculture, National Agricultural Statistics Service, "USDA Historical Track Records," (Washington, D.C.: United States Government Printing Office, 2005), 133, 141.

257 Ibid., 20, 116, 123, 204.

258 Cattle Fax, "Omaha Prices: Fat Steers, 1940–2007," http://www.cattlefax.com/data/files/beef/omahastrprice.xls, retrieved December 20, 2007.

[259] Jason Manning, "The Eighties Club: The Politics and Pop Culture of the 1980s: The Midwest Farm Crisis of the 1980s," http://eighiesclub.tripod.com/id395.htm, retrieved January 24, 2007.

[260] Ibid.

[261] Ibid.

[262] Ibid.

[263] Ibid. The farm crisis of the 1980s has been studied extensively, although much remains to be done. For explorations of the subject see, R. Douglas Hurt, *American Agriculture: A Brief History* (Ames: Iowa State University Press, 1994); Osha Gray Davidson, *Broken Heartland: The Rise of America's Rural Ghetto* (New York: The Free Press, 1990); Bruce L. Gardner, *American Agriculture in the Twentieth Century: How it Flourished and What it Cost* (Cambridge: Harvard University Press, 2002); Dennis S. Nordin and Roy V. Scott, *From Prairie Farmer to Entrepreneur: The Transformation of Midwestern Agriculture* (Bloomington: Indiana University Press, 2005), and James Corcoran, *Bitter Harvest: Gordon Kahl and the Posse Comitatus: Murder in the Heartland* (New York: Penguin, 1990), among others.

[264] Manning.

[265] Ibid.

[266] Joseph A. Amato, *The Great Jerusalem Artichoke Circus: The Buying and Selling of the Rural American Dream* (St. Paul: University of Minnesota Press, 1993); Jim Hightower, *Hard Tomatoes Hard Times: The Hightower Report* (New York: Hippocrene Books, 1978).

[267] Manning.

[268] Manning.

[269] Hugh Sidey, *Time*, August 11, 1986, 15.

[270] Link, "Guardian of the Land: Arthur A. Link," 38.

[271] Ibid., 38–39.

[272] State of North Dakota, State Canvassing Board, "Official Abstract of Votes Cast at the General Election Held November 5, 1980".

[273] Ibid.; William A. DeGregorio, *The Complete Book of U.S. Presidents: From Washington to Bill Clinton*, 4th edition (New York: Wings Books, 1993), 644.

[274] National Oceanic and Atmospheric Administration, "Climate at a Glance: Annual Precipitation: North Dakota," http://climvis.ncdc.noaa.gov/ccgi-bin/cag3/hr-display3.pl, retrieved November 29, 2007.

[275] Karissa A. Haugeberg, "A Legal Response to Legislative Failure: *ARC v North Dakota*," Honors Thesis, University of North Dakota, 2000, 11–13. Haugeberg's essay is by far the best exploration of the Grafton State School scandal.

[276] Ibid., 16.

[277] Ibid., 20.

[278] Ibid., 23–24.

[279] Ibid., 26, 28.

[280] Ibid., 31–32.

[281] Ibid., 35–36.

[282] Ibid., 39–40.

[283] Corcoran, 26–30. For more on the Posse Comitatus, see Kenneth S. Stern, *A Force Upon the Plain: The American Militia Movement and the Politics of Hate* (New York: Simon and Schuster, 1996); Catherine McNicol Stock, *Rural Radicals: From Bacon's Rebellion to the*

Oklahoma City Bombing (New York: Penguin, 1996); Capstan Turner with Jay Lowery, *There Was a Man: The Saga of Gordon Kahl: A True Story* (Nashville, TN: Sozo Publishing, 1995), to name but a few. Also worthy of reading for an understanding of the radicalized farm movement and the Christian Identity movement is Daniel Levitas, *The Terrorist Next Door: The Militia Movement and the Radical Right* (New York: Thomas Dunne Books, 2002).

284 Corcoran, 29–31.

285 Corcoran, 75–105. The story told by Turner and Lowery, as well as by Darrell Graf and Steve Schnabel, *It's All About Power: A True and Accurate Eye-Witness Account of the Shoot-out Between Gordon Kahl and US Marshals at Medina, North Dakota* (Fargo: MPD, Inc., 1999) differs significantly in interpretation from that offered by Corcoran. However, as Turner and Lowery's work is from the position of the Christian Identity movement and finds no fault with Kahl, and Graf and Schnabel's labor is from the perspective of two Medina police officers involved in the arrest attempt, Corcoran's version of the story, the least biased of those examined, will be hewed to in this brief account.

286 Corcoran, 184–211, 233–46.

287 North Dakota State Data Center, *North Dakota Population Projections: 2005 to 2020*, Table A. "Populations Trends in North Dakota by County: 1980–2020," (Fargo: North Dakota State Data Center, 2000), vi.

288 Ibid.

289 Bureau of Business and Economic Research, "North Dakota Crude Oil Production, 1951–1978," Table 9.05, *Statistical Abstract of North Dakota, 1979* (University of North Dakota: Grand Forks, 1979), 347; Ben Meier, Secretary of State, *North Dakota Centennial Blue Book, 1889–1989* (n.p., n.d.), 530.

290 Tweton and Jelliff, 176–77; United States Department of Commerce, *1980 Census of Population.* Vol. I, Characteristics of the Population, Part 36, North Dakota. (Washington, D.C.: United States Government Printing Office, 1983), Table 217, "Detailed Occupation of the Experienced Civilian Labor Force and Employed Person by Sex: 1980 and 1970," 36–56.

291 Larry Woiwode, *Aristocrat of the West: The Story of Harold Schafer* (Fargo: North Dakota Institute for Regional Studies, 2000). For overviews of the state's economy during the last half-century see, Scot Arthur Stradley, *The Broken Circle: An Economic History of North Dakota* (Grand Forks, ND: Bureau of Business and Economic Research, 1993) and Lowell R. Goodman, *The Economic Health of North Dakota* (Grand Forks, ND: LRG Ltd., with the University of North Dakota Alumni Association, 1996).

292 North Dakota Legislative Council, "Formation of a North Dakota Gaming Commission: Background Memorandum," Judiciary Committee, September 2007.

293 Ibid.; Link, 44.

294 State of North Dakota, State Canvassing Board, "Official Abstract of Votes Cast at the General Election Held November 2, 1982".

295 State of North Dakota, State Canvassing Board, "Official Abstract of Votes Cast at the General Election Held November 2, 1982"; Rathke, 201.

296 State of North Dakota, State Canvassing Board, "Official Abstract of Votes Cast at the General Election Held November 6, 1984"; *New York Times*, January 3, 1985; Shoptaugh, 197–99. Sinner had at one time contemplated becoming a priest, spending six years in seminary before determining that the priesthood was not his true calling. See Justin Schardin, "The HPR Governor Series: Gov. George Sinner, 1985–1992," *High Plains Reader*, November 11, 2007, 8–9.

[297] State of North Dakota, State Canvassing Board, "Official Abstract of Votes Cast at the General Election Held November 6, 1984".

[298] Dennis S. Nordin and Roy V. Scott, *From Prairie Farmer to Entrepreneur: The Transformation of Midwestern Agriculture* (Bloomington: Indiana University Press, 2005, 194–96; R. Douglas Hurt, *American Agriculture: A Brief History* (Ames: Iowa State University Press, 1994), 356; see as well Osha Gray Davidson, *Broken Heartland: The Rise of America's Rural Ghetto* (New York: The Free Press, 1990); Bruce L. Gardner, *American Agriculture in the Twentieth Century: How it Flourished and What it Cost* (Cambridge: Harvard University press, 2002).

[299] With regard to the continuing farm crisis, see Nordin and Scott, Hurt, as well as, Davidson, *Broken Heartland*; Bruce L. Gardner, *American Agriculture in the Twentieth Century: How it Flourished and What it Cost* (Cambridge: Harvard University press, 2002); and James Corcoran, *Bitter Harvest: Gordon Kahl and the Posse Comitatus: Murder in the Heartland* (New York: Penguin, 1990), among others. United States Department of Agriculture, National Agricultural Statistics Service,

[300] Jerome E. Johnson, "Farmland Values Declined More in 1984," North Dakota Farm Research, Vol. 47.4 (January-February 1990), 23.

[301] Ibid., 26.

[302] United States Department of Agriculture, National Agricultural Statistics Service, "USDA Historical Track Records," (Washington, D.C.: United States Government Printing Office, 2005), 20, 116, 123.

[303] Ibid., 132, 141, 204.

[304] Cattle Fax, "Omaha Prices: Fat Steers, 1940–2007," http://www.cattle-fax.com/data/files/beef/omahastrprice.xls, retrieved December 20, 2007.

[305] Randal C. Coon and F. Larry Leistritz, "Economic Contribution North Dakota Cooperatives Make to the State Economy," *Ag Issues*, http://www.crystalsugar.com/agronomy/resources/whitepapers/files/econ.asp, retrieved August 3, 2006; Calamity Pictures, "Where Have All the Children Gone," 1996; Turner Broadcasting, "Portrait of America: North Dakota," 1984.

[306] Andrea Domaskin, "Chasing the Bucks: Fee Hunting in North Dakota," Honors Essay, University of North Dakota, 2003; see as well Great Plains Institute for Sustainable Development, *Renewing the Countryside: North Dakota* (Minneapolis: Great Plains Institute for Sustainable Development/Northern Great Plains, Inc., 2003), 148–51.

[307] *Renewing the Countryside: North Dakota*, 148–51.

[308] Ibid., 38–41.

[309] Tara Williams-Sether, Kathleen M. Macek-Rowland and Douglas G. Emerson, "Climatic and Hydrologic Aspects of the 1988–1992 Drought and the Effect on People and Resources of North Dakota," North Dakota Water Commission, Water Resources Investigation 29.

[310] Ibid.

[311] Kimberly K. Porter, *Uncommon Heroes: The City of Grand Forks Flood Fight, 1997* (Grand Forks: North Dakota Museum of Art, 2001), 11.

[312] United States Department of Commerce, *1990 Census of Population*. General Population Characteristics, North Dakota. Table 1 "Summary of General Characteristics of Persons: 1990" (Washington, D.C.: United States Government Printing Office, 1992.

[313] North Dakota State Data Center, "North Dakota Population Projections: 2005 to 2020," Population Estimates and Projections, http://www.ndsu.edu/sdc/data/populationtrends.htm, retrieved November 30, 2007.

[314] Ibid.

[315] Ibid.

[316] Deborah Epstein Popper and Frank J. Popper, "The Great Plains: From Dust to Dust," *Planning* 53 (12, December 1987): 12–18.

[317] Ibid.

[318] Ibid.

[319] Alvin A. Jaeger, Secretary of State, *North Dakota Blue Book, 1995* (Bismarck, ND: n.p., 1995), 525–530.

[320] Ibid., 530–33.

[321] Ben Meier, Secretary of State, *North Dakota Centennial Blue Book, 1889–1989* (n.p., n.d.), 519.

[322] Ibid., 531.

[323] Ibid.; Gerald G. Newborg, editor, "Guardian of the Land: Arthur A. Link," *North Dakota History*, 72. 1 and 2: 25.

[324] Basin Electric Power Company, "Natural Gas," http://www.basinelectric.com/EnergyResources/Gas/, retrieved December 31, 2007.

[325] State of North Dakota, State Canvassing Board, "Official Abstract of Votes Cast at the General Election Held November 5, 1980"; State of North Dakota, State Canvassing Board, "Official Abstract of Votes Cast at the General Election Held November 7, 1972"; State of North Dakota, State Canvassing Board, "Official Abstract of Votes Cast at the General Election Held November 4, 1986".

[326] State of North Dakota, State Canvassing Board, "Official Abstract of Votes Cast at the General Election Held November 4, 1986".

[327] Ben Meier, Secretary of State, *North Dakota Centennial Blue Book, 1889–1989* (n.p., n.d.), 378–430, 136; Ann M. Rathke, "Lady, If You Go Into Politics: North Dakota's Women Legislators, 1923–1989," unpublished M.A. Thesis, University of North Dakota, 1990.

[328] State of North Dakota, State Canvassing Board, "Official Abstract of Votes Cast at the General Election Held November 8, 1988".

[329] Ibid.

[330] Kathryn R.L. Rand and Steven Andrew Light, *Indian Gaming Law and Policy* (Durham, NC: Carolina Academic Press, 2006), 35.

[331] Alvin A. Jaeger, Secretary of State, *North Dakota Blue Book, 1995* (Bismarck, ND: n.p., 1995), 472.

[332] Ibid.

[333] Link, 72. 1 and 2: 42–43; Alvin A. Jaeger, Secretary of State, *North Dakota Blue Book, 1995* (Bismarck, ND: n.p., 1995), 440–41.

[334] Ibid.

[335] Patrick J. Brown, editor, *The People Celebrate: A Report on North Dakota's Centennial* (n.p., n.d.), 79–80.

[336] Ibid., 80–81.

[337] United States Department of Commerce, *1990 Census of Population*. General Population Characteristics, North Dakota. Table 1 "Summary of General Characteristics of Persons: 1990" (Washington, D.C.: United States Government Printing Office, 1992); United States

Department of Commerce, *1980 Census of Population*. Vol. I, Characteristics of the Population, Part 36, North Dakota. (Washington, D.C.: United States Government Printing Office, 1983).

338 Richard L. Forstall, compiler and editor, "North Dakota: Population of Counties by Decennial Census: 1900 to 1990," (1995), http://www.census.gov/population/cencounts/nd190090.txt, retrieved December 17, 2007.

339 Ibid.; for an interesting exploration of depopulation in Slope County see Zachary Karsky: "Slope County: A Review of Rural Depopulation and Change," Honors Essay, University of North Dakota, 2007.

340 United States Department of Commerce, *1990 Census of Population*. General Population Characteristics, North Dakota. Table 1 "Summary of General Characteristics of Persons: 1990" (Washington, D.C.: United States Government Printing Office, 1992).

341 Ibid.

342 Ibid.; United States Department of Commerce, *1980 Census of Population*. Vol. I, Characteristics of the Population, Part 36, North Dakota. Table 15, "Persons by Race," (Washington, D.C.: United States Government Printing Office, 1983).

343 United States Department of Commerce, *1980 Census of Population*. Vol. I, Characteristics of the Population, Part 36, North Dakota. Table 15, "Persons by Race," (Washington, D.C.: United States Government Printing Office, 1983); United States Department of Commerce, *1990 Census of Population*. General Population Characteristics, North Dakota. Table 3 "Race and Hispanic Origin: 1990," 1 "Summary of General Characteristics of Persons: 1990" (Washington, D.C.: United States Government Printing Office, 1992).

344 Ibid., Table 13, "Race and Hispanic Origin for American Indian and Alaska Native Areas: 1990".

345 United States Department of Agriculture, National Agricultural Statistics Service, "Total Farms, Land in Farms, Average Farm Size," http://www.nass.usda.gov/QuickStats/PullData_US.jsp, retrieved January 2, 2008

346 Osha Gray Davidson, *Broken Heartland: The Rise of America's Rural Ghetto* (New York: Free Press, 1990).

347 Nordin and Scott, 203–05.

348 United States Department of Agriculture, National Agricultural Statistics Service, "USDA Historical Track Records," (Washington, D.C.: United States Government Printing Office, 2005), 20, 46, 116, 123.

349 Ibid., 132, 141, 204; Cattle Fax, "Omaha Prices: Fat Steers, 1940–2007," http://www.cattle-fax.com/data/files/beef/omahastrprice.xls, retrieved December 20, 2007.

350 North Dakota Agricultural Statistics Service, "1995 North Dakota County Rents and Values," April 1995.

351 NDSU Extension Service, "The Myths and Realities of North Dakota Poverty: It's Everybody's Business," May 1992.

352 Great Plains Institute for Sustainable Development, *Renewing the Countryside: North Dakota* (Minneapolis: Great Plains Institute for Sustainable Development/Northern Great Plains, Inc., 2003), 64–71.

353 Larry Fruhling, "Nebraskans Fire on 'Buffalo Commons' Idea," *Des Moines Sunday Register* 1A, 6A.

354 Lowell R. Goodman, *The Economic Health of North Dakota* (Grand Forks, ND: LRG Properties, Ltd., 1996), 282–83.

355 Ibid., 274–75.

356 Ibid., 282.

357 Scot Arthur Stradley, *The Broken Circle: An Economic History of North Dakota* (Grand Forks, ND: Bureau of Business and Economic Research, 1993).

358 Ibid., Dorreen Yellow Bird, "Viewpoints in Conflict," *Grand Forks Herald*, November 22, 1997, B1.

359 Steven Andrew Light and Kathryn R.L. Rand, "Within Boundaries: Indian Gaming in North Dakota and Beyond," essay to be published in *Gambling, Space, and Time*, ed. Paulina Raento and David Schwartz (Reno: University of Nevada, forthcoming 2009), draft page 21.

360 Ibid.; James Lam, "Evaluating the Impact of Federal Welfare Reform Legislation in Indian Country: A Policy Guide for the Standing Rock Sioux Tribe," (Cambridge, MA: Harvard, May 1997), 10; Mary Jane Schneider, *North Dakota Indians: An Introduction* (Dubuque, IA: Kendall/Hunt, 1994), 204–05.

361 Ibid.

362 United States Department of Energy, National Renewable energy Laboratory, Division of Community Services, "Wind Powering America," pamphlet DOE/GO-102000-0992, April 2000.

363 North Dakota Department of Economic Development and Finance, "Growing North Dakota," video, 1992.

364 State of North Dakota, State Canvassing Board, "Official Abstract of Votes Cast at the General Election Held November 6, 1990".

365 Sarah Coomber, "Blue Law Backers Fought Opening with Great Vigor," *Fargo Forum*, August 29, 1999, 1A.

366 Ibid.

367 Ibid.

368 Alvin A. Jaeger, *North Dakota Blue Book, 1995* (Bismarck, ND: n.p., 1995), 115.

369 Ibid.; State of North Dakota, State Canvassing Board, "Official Abstract of Votes Cast at the General Election Held November 3, 1992".

370 Ibid.

371 Ibid.

372 Jaeger, 115–16; ibid.; State of North Dakota, State Canvassing Board, "Official Abstract of Votes Cast at the Special Election Held December 4, 1992".

373 State of North Dakota, State Canvassing Board, "Official Abstract of Votes Cast at the General Election Held November 8, 1994".

374 North Dakota State Data Center, "Population Estimates for North Dakota by County, 1990–1999," *The Population Bulletin*, Vol. 16.4 (April 2000).

375 Ibid.

376 Ibid.

377 North Dakota State Data Center, "Median Age in North Dakota by County (in years): 1950 to 2000," *The Population Bulletin*, Vol. 17.6 (June 2001).

378 North Dakota State Data Center, "Population Estimates for North Dakota by County, 1990–1999," *The Population Bulletin*, Vol. 16.4 (April 2000).

379 Federation for American Immigration Reform, "North Dakota Immigrant Admissions," http://www.fairus.org/site/PageServer?pagename=research_researche096, retrieved November 5, 2007.

[380] United States Department of Agriculture, National Agricultural Statistics Service, "Total Farms, Land in Farms, Average Farm Size," http://www.nass.usda.gov/QuickStats/PullData_US.jsp, retrieved January 2, 2008.

[381] North Dakota Agricultural Statistics Service, USDA, "North Dakota at a Glance," November 2004.

[382] North Dakota Department of Agriculture, Testimony, United States House of Representatives, June 29, 2000, http://www.agdepartment.com/Testimony/Testimony%202000/test000629.html, retrieved April 21, 2008.

[383] Ibid.

[384] Ibid.

[385] United States Department of Agriculture, National Agricultural Statistics Service, "USDA Historical Track Records," (Washington, D.C.: United States Government Printing Office, 2005), 20, 46, 116, 123.

[386] Ibid., 132, 141, 204; Cattle Fax, "Omaha Prices: Fat Steers, 1940–2007," http://www.cattle-fax.com/data/files/beef/omahastrprice.xls, retrieved December 20, 2007.

[387] See Great Plains Institute for Sustainable Development, *Renewing the Countryside: North Dakota* (Minneapolis: Great Plains Institute for Sustainable Development/Northern Great Plains, Inc., 2003) for assorted efforts to keep rural North Dakota vital.

[388] For a discussion of rural women working in town to help support the family farming/ranching operation see Deborah Fink, *Open Country Iowa: Rural Women, Tradition and Change* (Albany: State University of New York, 1986), 233–37; Deborah Fink, *Cutting into the Meatpacking Line: Workers and Change in the Rural Midwest* (Chapel Hill: University of North Carolina Press, 1998), 78–80; David Sutherland Productions in conjunction with Frontline, "The Farmer's Wife," (film) 1998; Jeanne Jordan and Steven Ascher, "Troublesome Creek: A Midwestern," (film), American Experience, 1995; James Corcoran, *Bitter Harvest: Gordon Kahl and the Posse Comitatus: Murder in the Heartland* (New York: Penguin, 1990), 11–14.

[389] Gail Hogan, "Three counties, four pastors, eight churches, one ministry," *Grand Forks Herald*, February 8, 1997, 7A; Calamity Pictures, "Where Have All the Children Gone," 1996.

[390] Tom Decker, "North Dakota Demographics: How Our Changing Population Will Impact Elementary and Secondary Education," Department of Public Instruction, 2007.

[391] Ibid.; in 2007, 195 school districts existed in the state. Numbers are expected to continue their decline over the foreseeable future.

[392] Ibid.

[393] Randy Bradbury, "Seeking brighter Futures: Many of North Dakota's brainiest young people see little opportunity for themselves in the state," *Grand Forks Herald*, January 5, 1997, Section C.

[394] Jayne Clark, "Dakota moments," *USA TODAY*, August 29, 2001, Section D, 1–2.

[395] For more about Indian gaming see Rand and Light.

[396] Ibid.

[397] United States Bureau of the Census, "Manufacturing Employment and Pay by State, 2001-2004," *Annual Survey of Manufacturers*, http://www.ssti.org/Digest/Tables/032006t.htm, retrieved March 23, 2007; North Dakota Department of Economic Development and Finance, "Growing North Dakota," video, 1992.

398 Kate Spilde, "Indian Gaming in North Dakota: Resisting the Exodus," NIGA Resource Library, 2000, http://www.indiangaming.org/library/articles/north-dakota.shtml, retrieved November 13, 2007.

399 Alvin A. Jaeger, *North Dakota Blue Book, 1997–1999* (Bismarck, ND: n.p., 1997), 506–10.

400 Energy Information Administration, State Energy Profiles, "North Dakota," http://tonto.eia.doe.gov/state/state_energy_profiles.cfm?sid=ND, Retrieved April 7, 2008.

401 Alvin A. Jaeger, *North Dakota Blue Book, 1997–1999* (Bismarck, ND: n.p., 1997), 511–15.

402 Great Plains Institute for Sustainable Development, *Renewing the Countryside: North Dakota* (Minneapolis: Great Plains Institute for Sustainable Development/Northern Great Plains, Inc., 2003), 100–03; United States Department of Energy, National Renewable energy Laboratory, Division of Community Services, "Wind Powering America," pamphlet DOE/GO-102000-0992, April 2000.

403 Alvin A. Jaeger, *North Dakota Blue Book, 1997–1999* (Bismarck, ND: n.p., 1997), 577–78.

404 Ibid.; Porter, 11.

405 Staff of the Grand Forks Herald, *Come Hell and High Water: The Incredible Story of the 1997 Red River Flood* (Grand Forks: Grand Forks Herald, 1997), 38–40.

406 Ibid.

407 Ibid.; Alvin A. Jaeger, *North Dakota Blue Book, 1997– 1999* (Bismarck, ND: n.p., 1997), 582–83.

408 Ibid., 583.

409 Bill Redekop, "Ill will swells with North Dakota water," *Winnipeg Free Press*, June 14, 2001, 1.

410 Ibid.; United States Geological Survey, North Dakota Water Science Center, "Devils Lake Basin," http://nd.water.usgs.gov/devilslake/, retrieved November 21, 2007.

411 State of North Dakota, State Canvassing Board, "Official Abstract of Votes Cast at the General Election Held November 5, 1996".

412 Ibid.

413 State of North Dakota, State Canvassing Board, "Official Abstract of Votes Cast at the General Election Held November 3, 1998".

414 Ibid.

415 University of North Dakota School of Medicine and Health Sciences, Center for Rural Health, *Rural Health Facts*, Spring 2006. Median age reflects 2004 statistic.

416 North Dakota State Data Center, "North Dakota Population Projections: 2005 to 2020," North Dakota State University (2005), v.

417 John Seewer, "An aging danger," *Grand Forks Herald*, July 2, 2007, 1–2.

418 National Priorities Project, "Federal Dollars: What Came to and Left Your State, 2005," http://www.nationalpriorities.org/Publications/What-Came-to-Your-State-in-2005.html, retrieved January 17, 2008.

419 Eric Sevareid, *Not So Wild a Dream: A Personal Story of Youth and War and the American Faith* (New York: Antheneum, 1976), 5.

420 Debra Marquart, *The Horizontal World: Growing Up Wild in the Middle of Nowhere* (New York: Counterpoint, 2006), 64. For more on outsiders' views of North Dakota see Ann Rathke, "The Image of North Dakota in Recent American Travel Literature," *North Dakota Quarterly* 56.4 (Fall 1988): 86–98; Wyonna H. wilkins, "The Idea of North Dakota," *North Dakota Quarterly*, 39.1 (Winter 1971): 5–28.